Improving the Army Planning, Programming, Budgeting, and Execution System (PPBES)

The Programming Phase

Leslie Lewis

Roger Allen Brown

John Y. Schrader

Prepared for the United States Army

RAND

Arroyo Center

For more information on the RAND Arroyo Center, contact the Director of Operations, (310) 393-0411, extension 6500, or visit the Arroyo Center's Web site at http://www.rand.org/organization/ard/

This project was part of a special assistance activity for the Director of the U.S. Army's Program Analysis and Evaluation Directorate (PA&E) conducted beginning in 1995 and continuing into 1997. The purpose of this project was to assist the Director of PA&E in creating a new program development process and methodology. The director's principal objective in this project was to improve the Army's Program Objective Memorandum (POM) development process. These improvements would be designed to (1) enhance the Army's ability to view the totality of its resources, (2) improve its resource decision process, and (3) justify those choices within the Army and to the external community, including the Office of the Secretary of Defense (OSD), the Chairman of the Joint Chiefs of Staff (CJCS), and the Congress.

The audience for this report primarily consists of those in the Department of Defense (DoD) involved in allocating resources to meet planned requirements.

The research was conducted in the Strategy, Doctrine, and Resources Program of the RAND Arroyo Center. The Arroyo Center is a federally funded research and development center sponsored by the United States Army.

CONTENTS

FIGURES

TABLES

INTRODUCTION

In September 1994, the Army Secretariat asked the Army Director of Program Analysis and Evaluation (DPA&E) to develop a POM process that involved the Secretariat in the resource decision process. The Secretariat also indicated that Management Decision Packages (MDEPs) needed to be linked to Army resource decisionmaking. In early 1995, the DPA&E asked RAND Arroyo Center how the Army might improve its resource allocation process and better justify its resources. The Arroyo Center was requested to devise a framework and methodology for the development of the Army POM 98-03 that would:

- Help the Army respond to the issues raised by the Secretariat;

- Provide linkage between MDEPs and Army resource decision-making;

- Ensure that proposed improvements could be implemented for POM 98-03.

The Arroyo Center's response was to create a comprehensive framework that addresses Army, OSD, and Joint Staff (JS) resource process concerns. It also ensures that the Army's demand for resources is balanced against its supply of available resources. The Arroyo Center determined that any proposed framework needed to be implemented incrementally for POM 98-03. Since 1995, many of these recommendations have been adopted; they will be summarized in the body of the report.

ARMY PROGRAMMING IN THE 1990s

The programming function allocates resources to requirements that achieve the national security objectives established in the planning phases of the DoD's Planning, Programming, and Budgeting System (PPBS) and the Army's Planning, Programming, Budgeting, and Execution System (PPBES). The programming function and related decisionmaking are centralized within the Army Headquarters staff but provide for inputs from Major Commands (MACOMs) and Program Executive Officers (PEOs). Within the Army Headquarters, several organizations develop requirements, allocate resources, and make resource decisions that result in the POM. Decisions on resource allocation are coupled with their corresponding rationale and linked to the strategy, objectives, and priorities from The Army Plan (TAP) and Defense Planning Guidance (DPG) with an assessment of their expected outputs.

The general consensus of judgments, both internal and external to the Army, was that Army POMs in the early 1990s, while being severely resource constrained, had not adequately resourced many established objectives and that resources had not been effectively balanced across high-priority requirements. While the Army had made some well-received improvements in the program-review hierarchy, such as creating the Army Resource Board (ARB) and its support group, these improvements had not been sufficient to eliminate both internal and external criticism. One persistent internal criticism was the lack of visibility of programming choices at various levels of the program hierarchy and throughout the programming process. The external DoD community had criticized the Army programming process for being internally focused and not adequately linked to the DoD and JS. The Army had presented the DPG as the basis for resource objectives but had rarely offered rationale as to how its programs met the needs of OSD and the commanders-in-chief (CINCs). In general, the Army was perceived as sacrificing the investment area to support force structure, readiness, and quality of life, often leading to the allocation of its total obligation authority (TOA) to more costly and less efficient programs.

THE NEW FRAMEWORK AND PROCESS

Several elements had to be considered in constructing a framework for Army programming. Joint requirements had to be integrated into Army decisionmaking. Resource choices had to be vetted both top down and bottom up. Tradeoff analyses had to be performed in a disciplined manner, and intertemporal issues had to be addressed within the tradeoffs. The sponsor also laid some ground rules:

• The Army MDEP structure would not be changed.

• The PROBE Database would remain the resource decision database.

• The Arroyo Center would address concepts for a resource decision architecture.

• Processes that affect Army resource requirements would be identified and their shortfalls would be discussed within Army-established constraints.

• Any proposed framework and process changes would support the Army's evolving Resource Campaign Strategy, an initiative to create a constrained approach to resource management that the Chief of Staff, Army asked the Assistant Vice Chief of Staff, Army (AVCSA) to develop. The AVCSA subsequently asked the Arroyo Center to help develop the Resource Campaign Strategy. Before this could be done, a number of tasks had to be completed, such as reengineering TAP. Recently, the Resource Campaign Strategy has evolved into the Army Strategic Resource Planning Process (ASRPP).

These requirements suggested that the Arroyo Center-developed Objectives-Based Planning Resource Management (OBPRM) would be a good starting point. The objective was to map Army issues into the broader joint framework through the identification of mission areas. A list of Army mission areas was constructed to capture the capabilities provided by the Army to combatant commanders. The mission areas were then linked to necessary objectives and tasks. The second element was the linkage of the orthogonal Army mission areas to the Title X functions. A three-tiered decision architecture that tied together the three major elements of the framework—principal Title X functions, major Army objectives, and the MDEPs—was proposed. The Title X functions provide the CINCs with the capabilities necessary to perform their joint missions.

The proposed resourcing framework is a process in which Army capabilities are assessed within the mission areas and programmed within the Title X functions. Ideally, this would be a repeatable process that provides a mechanism for the Army leadership to establish priorities and clearly defined, measurable objectives. It would link Army program choices to the joint warfighting objectives and national security goals. The linkage of functions to mission areas enables the Army to assess the total demand against available resources and simultaneously enhances the Army's ability to perform hierarchical tradeoff analyses and build options in a disciplined and repeatable manner.

IMPLEMENTATION OF NEW FRAMEWORK AND PROCESS

Before the proposed framework and process could be implemented, several changes needed to be made to accommodate DPA&E concerns about implementation during the FY98–03 POM cycle. The Army POM development processes existing in 1995 required modifications before they could support the proposed framework. The manner in which Program Evaluation Groups (PEGs) allocated resources and were assigned MDEPs also had to be changed. The PEG structure was redesigned, and the existing 14 panels were reengineered into the six broadly stated Title X summary functions critical to the Army.[1] The DPA&E wanted TAP to be incorporated into this process. Additionally, the DPA&E was concerned that the Army would not be able to implement a new process for the current POM. This necessitated an incremental implementation that avoided undue turbulence but indicated the leadership's concern with the current process.

It was determined that an OBPRM-like process would be developed that focused on adjusting PEG resource allocations. The process was composed of four levels: Army functional goals, which support the

---

[1] These Title X summary functions are Manning, Training, Equipping, Organizing, Sustaining, and Installations. These represent the twelve functions specifically addressed in statute.

six summary Title X functions; resource objectives; subobjectives; and tasks. Resource tasks were then linked to MDEPs. Resource task priorities were developed to ensure that PEGs would have sufficient guidance to support their allocation of resources. Priority I tasks are of fundamental importance to the overall achievement of the goals of the Army as an institution. Priority II tasks are important to the achievement of the key resource objectives within a primary function of the Army. Priority III tasks are important for enabling some portion or subsystem of a primary function of the Army. Priority IV tasks are of lesser importance than Priority I–III tasks and require either program visibility (i.e., in response to Army, OSD, CINC, or congressional special interest or directed guidance), close coordination among more than one PEG, or exchange of resource information with selected staff agencies and MACOMs.

An interactive spreadsheet connected to relational databases that contained the resource objectives and tasks was developed to guide the PEGs in developing and providing information on their review of requirements and, later, on their resource-allocation decisions among tasks and MDEPs. An assessment scale was developed to score each resource task:

A: Adequately resourced

P: Partially resourced

U: Unfunded.

Use of the relational databases allowed the review and analysis of resource allocations to individual resource tasks and MDEPs.

During the program development process, the outputs of the six PEGs were assessed within PA&E against joint operational requirements using the mission areas and their associated joint operational objectives and tasks. The DPA&E decided that, due to time constraints, the mission areas should be used only for internal Army assessments of how the PEG decisions met joint requirements. Qualitative assessments were provided to the Army to assist in the final adjudication of resources and to ensure that a balanced POM was developed. Subsequent expanded development of Army mission areas remained as an area for future effort.

LESSONS LEARNED AND NEXT STEPS

Generally, the participants in the revised POM process agreed that the Army needed to change its process and realign it to better reflect the current resource environment. Some criticisms of the revised process were identified and subsequently addressed by the Arroyo Center team:

- Limited audit trail of decisions and challenges to perceived organizational prerogatives;

- Lack of consistency across the PEGs in terms of resource objectives and tasks;

- Problems with the linkage of the MDEPs to the PEGs;

- Compressed Army POM schedule;

- Questionable future relevancy of TAP and the Army Programming Guidance Memorandum (APGM);

- Need for more participation of the Secretariat and MACOMs;

- Problems with coordination.

Further implementation of the proposed framework is planned to occur over subsequent years. However, soon after the programming process began, the DPA&E concluded that the revised PEG structure along the Title X functional areas was sufficient for this iteration of the POM. The DPA&E wanted to retain the six PEGs; structure the MDEPs to better accommodate the functional PEGs; and refine the resource goals, objectives, and tasks. The ODCSOPS and DPA&E agreed with the Arroyo Center project team recommendation that TAP should be redesigned in the future to include Army mission areas to provide better articulation of Army capability needs. The mission area assessment would identify how well the resource goals had been met within a PEG and also evaluate the total ability of the Army to provide required capabilities to joint force commanders.

Full implementation of the new framework and process would align the Army much closer with the realities of the OSD and Joint Staff resourcing processes and activities for the subsequent FY00–05 POM. When fully implemented, it would provide the Army the capability to assess resource allocation within the future joint context, evaluate these choices against the new capabilities being fielded in the next five to ten years, and ensure that the Army core competencies are sustained or modified in accordance with changes in the strategic environment. Our subsequent work will specifically focus on defining common standards and measures. We observed that many of the problems with the POM process could be eased if the Army maintained a continuous resource process throughout the year.

The POM process within the Army is responsive to OSD guidance and schedule, and the Army leadership recognizes that resource requirements and allocation are a main activity of the service headquarters. However, the development of key documents that provide resource guidance across the Army, which are integral to the implementation of a total resourcing framework and process, have not been consistent in practice. For instance, a vision document that could provide the Army some insights into what its leadership wants the Army to look like in the next 15 to 20 years was not published until 1996.[2] Strategic planning guidance that provides Army goals and objectives for the near-, mid-, and far-term has also been absent since early 1991. Work was initiated within ODCSOPS in 1997 to provide this guidance.[3] Similarly, a strategic resource plan could inform the Army on how the leadership intends to achieve the goals and objectives laid out in the vision incrementally over approximately the next 10 years or two POM cycles was not available. The strategic resource plan could provide priority guidance to the functional areas in terms of their respective resource objectives for the middle- to long-term; it could also define the standards and measures across the functional areas. An Army strategic resource plan would also provide the guidelines for the development of strategic resource plans for each of the functional areas. The DPA&E requested that the Arroyo Center project team develop the strategic resource plan. Initial work on this commenced in the fall of 1996.

---

[2]The Army Vision was promulgated by the Chief of Staff, Army, GEN Dennis J. Reimer in 1996 and expanded in Army Vision 2010 in 1997.

[3]The Army Strategic Planning Guidance (ASPG) has subsequently been published in 1998 and incorporated in TAP.

ACKNOWLEDGMENTS

The project team would like to thank a number of people. LTG David K. Heebner, the former Director of Army Program Analysis and Evaluation (DPA&E) and the current Assistant Vice Chief of Staff, Army (AVCSA), requested the initial work, supported it, and finally implemented (with modifications) the RAND-proposed framework and process. The former AVCSA, LTG Jay Garner (ret.), worked with the project team on various iterations of the process and recommended various courses of action for implementation. We would also like to thank COL Tom Molino (ret.), former Chief of the Strategic Plans and Policy Division (DAMO-SSP), and COL William H. Lord, Jr., former Chief of the Resource Analysis and Integration Office (DAMO-ZR) and now at the Army War College. Dr. Craig College, Deputy Director of PA&E, COL Patrick Bennett, Chief, Program Development Division (PA&E) and COL Greg Parlier, former Chief of Resource Planning and Analysis Division (PA&E) and now at the Recruiting Command, have continued to support the implementation of this work.

James Quinlivan deserves a special note of appreciation. He supported this work and allowed the project team significant latitude in defining an approach. His constructive comments and criticisms were useful in ensuring that an implementable framework and process were put forth. His continued support of the RAND Arroyo Center project team through each subsequent phase of implementation has been of great value.

The project team also thanks research assistants Mia Fromm, Anissa Thompson, and Matthew Gershwin for their assistance in all phases of this work.

ABBREVIATIONS

AAR	After Action Review
ACPC	Arroyo Center Policy Committee
APGM	Army Programming Guidance Memorandum
ARB	Army Resource Board
ARBSG	Army Resource Board Support Group
ARSTAF	Army Staff
ASA (FM&C)	Assistant Secretary of the Army (Financial Management and Comptroller)
ASA (RDA)	Assistant Secretary of the Army (Research, Development, and Acquisition)
ASPG	Army Strategic Planning Guidance
AVCSA	Assistant Vice Chief of Staff, Army
CINC	Commander-in-Chief
CJCS	Chairman, Joint Chiefs of Staff
COC	Council of Colonels
CORM	Commission on the Roles and Missions of the Armed Forces
CS	Combat Support
CSA	Chief of Staff, Army

CSS	Combat Service Support
DAB	Director of the Army Budget[†]
DAMO-ZR	Resource Analysis and Integration Office
DCSOPS	Deputy Chief of Staff for Operations and Plans
DCSOPS-FD	Deputy Chief of Staff for Operations and Plans–Force Development
DoD	Department of Defense
DPA&E	Director of Program Analysis and Evaluation
DPG	Defense Planning Guidance
DRB	Defense Resources Board
FFRDC	Federally Funded Research and Development Center
FYDP	Future Years Defense Program
IPL	Integrated Priority List
JROC	Joint Requirements Oversight Council
JS	Joint Staff
JWCA	Joint Warfighting Capabilities Assessment
LRAMP	Long Range Army Modernization Plan
MACOM	Major Command
MDEP	Management Decision Package
MRC	Major Regional Contingency
NMS	National Military Strategy
OBPRM	Objectives-Based Planning Resource Management
ODCSOPS	Office of the Deputy Chief of Staff for Operations and Plans

---

[†]In 1995, the Director of the Army Budget (DAB) was renamed as the Deputy Assistant Secretary of the Army for Army Budget (DASA-B).

OPTEMPO	Operating Tempo
OSD	Office of the Secretary of Defense
PA&E	Program Analysis and Evaluation
PBC	Program and Budget Committee
PDM	Program Decision Memorandum
PEG	Program Evaluation Group
PEO	Program Executive Officer
POC	Point of Contact
POM	Program Objective Memorandum
PPBES	Planning, Programming, Budgeting, and Execution System
PPBS	Planning, Programming, and Budgeting System
PRG	Program Review Group
PROBE	Program Optimization and Budget Evaluation
PSG	Prioritization Steering Group
SECDEF	Secretary of Defense
SELCOM	Select Committee
SES	Senior executive service
STRM	Strategies-to-tasks resource management
TAP	The Army Plan
TOA	Total Obligation Authority
TRADOC	Training and Doctrine Command
USA	Under Secretary of the Army
VCJCS	Vice Chairman, Joint Chiefs of Staff
VCSA	Vice Chief of Staff, Army

Chapter One

BACKGROUND AND PROJECT OVERVIEW

The Army, like all the military departments, is being confronted by fundamentally changed strategic and resource environments. Requests for resources are increasingly being questioned because of continuing reductions in defense expenditures (beginning 1987) and the collapse of the Soviet Union (1991). The Goldwater-Nichols legislation, passed in 1986,[1] provided increased civilian management of the Department of Defense (DoD) and ensured that joint military judgment was an important part of all resource and operational decisionmaking. The level of detailed involvement by the Office of the Secretary of Defense (OSD) and the Joint Staff (JS) with review of the services' resource priorities has increased significantly since the passage of this legislation, as evidenced by reviewing the Chairman's Program Assessment (CPA), the Chairman's Program Recommendation (CPR), work done by the Joint Requirements Oversight Council (JROC), and emphasis given to program responses to the combatant commanders Integrated Priority Lists (IPLs).

The management model used in the Goldwater-Nichols legislation is centralized planning and decentralized execution. The OSD provides direction and guidance based on U.S. national security objectives. The commanders-in-chief (CINCs) request capabilities through the CINC requirements process. The military departments provide the resources for needed capabilities, as defined by their

---

[1]Public Law 99-433, October 1, 1986.

1

Title X functions.[2] The Chairman of the Joint Chiefs of Staff (CJCS) and the OSD integrate and balance CINC demands and service programs. In particular, the Goldwater-Nichols legislation redefined the role of the CJCS (and by default his staff) to include responsible prioritization of CINC requirements. The CJCS represents those requirements in the planning and programming phases of the Planning, Programming, and Budgeting System (PPBS). OSD is formally empowered by Title X to review and modify service program decisions. These functions are underpinned by revised versions of several existing resource identification and management processes—requirements, PPBS, JROC, and acquisition—and the development of new ones, such as the Joint Warfighting Capabilities Assessment (JWCA).[3]

In September 1994, the Army Secretariat informed the Army Director of Program Analysis and Evaluation (DPA&E) that it wanted a Program Objective Memorandum (POM) process that involved the Secretariat more in the resource decision process.[4] The Army's Management Decision Packages (MDEPs) were to be more closely linked to Army resource decisionmaking.[5] The Secretariat noted that the

---

[2]The Title X functions are the following: recruiting; organizing; supplying; equipping; training; servicing; mobilizing; demobilizing; administering; maintaining; constructing, outfitting, and repairing military equipment; constructing, maintaining, and repairing buildings, structures, and utilities; and acquiring real property and interests in real property necessary to carry out the responsibilities specified. Public Law 99-433, October 1, 1986.

[3]The JWCA is a relatively new process and is an outgrowth of the JROC's responsibilities to identify operational shortfalls of the CINCs and determine which service proposals could solve the shortfall. Leslie Lewis and others have done extensive work on the JWCA and were instrumental in hosting a conference on military overseas presence and its relationship to the JWCA. JWCA was initiated in 1994 to assist the Vice Chairman of the Joint Chiefs of Staff (VCJCS) in identifying the CINCs' priorities and their operational shortfalls for the near, middle, and long terms.

[4]Army Assistant Secretary's internal Army memorandum, to PA&E, September 14, 1995. An internal Army study sponsored by the Secretariat also identified a number of problems in how the Secretariat and Army Major Commands (MACOMs) participate in the PPBS process.

[5]MDEPs describe a complete activity or program, the resources required or allocated to perform the program throughout the budget and program years of the Future Years Defense Program (FYDP), and the listing of staff action personnel responsible for or interested in that program. The MDEP usually covers all appropriations required to execute the entire program.

current MDEP structure was too cumbersome and failed to provide a clear audit trail of resource decisions.

ARMY PROGRAMMING: PRE-1996 OVERVIEW[6]

Overview

Programming is a major function within the Army's resource management and decisionmaking process: the Planning, Programming, Budgeting, and Execution System (PPBES). The purpose of Army programming is "to distribute available manpower, dollars, and materiel among competing requirements per Army resource allocation policy and priorities" (U.S. Army War College, 1995, p. 14-11; Headquarters, Department of the Army, 1994). The programming function allocates resources to requirements and capabilities that achieve the national security objectives and priorities established in the planning phases of DoD PPBS and Army PPBES. Decisions on resource allocation complete the programming phase. In addition, resource allocation decisions are the foundation of the budgeting phase, during which the needed resources are obtained from Congress (U.S. Army War College, 1995, Ch. 14).

Pre-1996 Organization of Army Programming

The programming function and related decisionmaking are centralized within the Army Headquarters staff but allow inputs from Major Commands (MACOMs), which are the principal field operating agencies, and from Program Executive Officers (PEOs), who are the materiel developers. The Assistant Secretary of the Army (Financial Management and Comptroller) (ASA [FM&C]) provides oversight for the entire PPBES, and the DPA&E is responsible for the programming phase of the process. Several formal and informal organizations within Army Headquarters assist DPA&E in developing and reviewing requirements, allocating resources, and helping the Army leadership make the resource decisions that result in the POM. The POM is the official documentation of Army resource decisions and is the primary input to the DoD program review and issue cycle process.

---

[6]For a complete history of Army programming and its organization, see Appendix A.

We describe the organization of Army programming in the following section.

Organizational Elements

Several organizational elements are involved in programming at Army Headquarters by being resident on the staff or sending representatives (Army Regulation 1-1: Planning, Programming, Budgeting, and Execution System, 1994, Ch. 2 and 4):

- **MDEPs** are the records through which the Army records decisions on resource allocation for various program activities. MDEP Points of Contact (POCs) or managers are the staff proponents for each record.

- **PEGs** are organized by staff function, responsibility, and major programs. The principal function of these groups is to allocate resources to MDEPs assigned to them by DPA&E. Through 1995, the Army had 14 PEGs.

- **The Council of Colonels (COC)** is an ad hoc body representing all major headquarters staff functions that assists in preparation, execution, and review of the programming function.

- **MACOMs** are the principal field operating agencies, and **PEOs** are the principal acquisition agents of the Army. These two groups provide inputs into the PPBES to establish requirements and ultimately execute the resulting budgets.

- **The Program and Budget Committee (PBC)** is the Army's PPBES oversight, review, and executive advisory organization. Its members are from the ARSTAF and Secretariat at the General Officer and Senior Executive Service (SES) level.

- **The PSG** is chaired by the Deputy Chief of Staff for Operations and Plans (DCSOPS) and is composed of the ARSTAF members at the Lieutenant General and invited Secretariat observers usually at the Assistant Secretary level. It reviews the programming output of the PBC.

- **The SELCOM** (Select Committee) provided senior executive oversight on all PPBES and major policy matters, reviewed key issues, and recommended decisions to the Army senior leadership. The committee was jointly chaired by the Under Secretary of the Army and the VCSA. The SELCOM was eliminated in 1995 and replaced by the Army Resource Board (ARB).

— **ARB** performs the same functions previously assigned to the SELCOM but with streamlined membership and the inclusion of the senior Army decisionmakers. There is also an ad hoc Army Resource Board Support Group (ARBSG), which informs, coordinates, discusses, reviews, and advises the ARB members on headquarters PPBES and policy matters. The ARB is composed of the Secretary of the Army; Under Secretary; Assistant Secretaries; Chief of Staff, Army (CSA); Vice Chief of Staff, Army (VCSA); and the DCSOPS. The Secretary of the Army chairs the ARB.[7]

— **Senior Army Decisionmakers** include the Secretary of the Army, the CSA, the Under Secretary of the Army (USA), and the VCSA. The Secretary, with the advice of the CSA, approves the Army POM.

1995 ORGANIZATIONAL CHANGES

Following the recommendations of a 1995 Army Secretariat Special Review, the Blumenfeld Study, the Secretary of the Army implemented some major changes to the headquarters management and review organization. Figure 1.1 shows the Army program organization following the restructuring in 1995. The key changes affecting the programming function were the elimination of the SELCOM, seldom employed as a true deliberative body but more often used as

---

[7]The membership of the ARB has evolved since this research and now appears to include the Assistant VCSA. Further, the Director of PA&E is often included as a non-voting participant who provides program and resource information to the membership. Further, the ARB Support Group (ARBSG) was created to provide a forum, absent the senior Army leadership, that provides review, issue coordination, and recommendations on all phases of the Army PPBES to the ARB. The ARBSG is chaired by the Assistant Secretary of the Army for Financial Management and Comptroller (ASA (FM&C)). The membership of the ARBSG includes all Assistant Secretaries of the Army, the General Counsel, DCSOPS, DPA&E, Deputy Assistant Secretary for the Army Budget (DAB), and the Special Assistant to the ASA (FM&C)/ARB Executive Secretary. The use and influence of the ARBSG on Army PPBES has increased significantly since its initial activation in 1996. AR 11-32 provides the existing PPBES review process and organization.

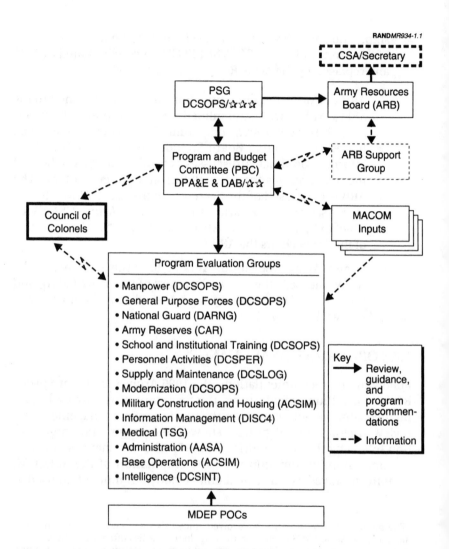

RAND*MR934-1.1*

Figure 1.1—Army Program Hierarchy 1995[8]

---

[8]In 1995, the SELCOM was replaced by the ARB and subsequently the ARBSG was created. The ARBSG organization was officially chartered by ASA (FM&C) memorandum in early 1996. During the programming phase of POM 98-03 the ARBSG initiated activities to coordinate resource allocation issues requiring ARB approval. In subsequent years, the ARBSG has functioned as an hierarchical body that reviews the recommendations of both the PBC and PSG.

an information forum, and the creation of the ARB. The ARB performs more active review and decision functions focused on resources but inclusive of the entire Army PPBES than those previously assigned to the SELCOM and with a streamlined membership that includes the senior Army decisionmakers. These changes provided increased civilian leadership involvement and visibility of the PPBES and related policy matters, but elimination of the SELCOM also reduced the direct involvement in resource matters of several senior military staff principals including the deputy and assistant chiefs of staff except for the DCSOPS. Other PPBES organizations, such as the PBC, were retained without changes in function.

Shortly after the creation of the formally constituted ARB, another PPBES, policy review, and executive-advisory group was formed on an ad hoc basis, called the ARBSG. Its initial and continuing purpose is to inform, coordinate, discuss, review, and advise the ARB members on headquarters PPBES issues and policy matters before their formal presentation to the ARB.

The Army Programming Process

Army programming is an ordered, event- and schedule-driven, hierarchical decision process. The process is centrally managed at the Army Headquarters with input from the MACOMs and PEOs that will ultimately execute many of the programs that Congress approves for funding in the budget. The process is normally initiated with senior Army leadership approval of TAP, which in Section III provides specific objectives, program priorities, and resource guidance for programming.[9] TAP employs an iterative method of establishing requirements and providing guidance and priorities to PEGs, which are responsible for interpreting TAP guidance and performing the detailed allocation of resources against requirements within their areas of responsibility, also detailed in the form of MDEPs.

Each PEG resource allocation iteration is reviewed by oversight organizations, such as the PBC, that give detailed guidance to the PEGs

---

[9]Section III of TAP is titled the Army Programming Guidance Memorandum (APGM). The APGM is developed within the Directorate for Program Evaluation and Analysis (PA&E).

and adjust resource allocations to balance the broader program. After several iterations, the process identifies key resource issues, usually those requirements or programs that are not allocated sufficient resources to achieve their stated objectives, for discussion, guidance, and option development at a higher level. The process progresses through the oversight hierarchy, with each separate level attempting to winnow the issues until only a small number remain. These issues are then presented to the Army leadership with recommendations for decision. Options for addressing the final few issues are provided, and decisions are normally made that result in the resource allocation presented in the POM.

Throughout this programming process, the DPA&E is responsible for maintaining a current and timely record of the resource allocation decisions in the Program Optimization and Budget Evaluation (PROBE) database. The PROBE database is a fiscally constrained tool that iteratively records Army programming decisions and provides visibility of Program Elements (PEs), MDEPs, and resources, i.e., funds by appropriation and manpower. The DPA&E is also empowered to analyze and evaluate the activities of the PEGs and PBC, assist in the development of program options to respond to issues, and oversee the balance of resource decisions between competing requirements, programs, and priorities established by the DCSOPS.

Evaluating the Output of Programming

External to the Army, the POM is explicitly evaluated on the basis of the level of resourcing provided to a number of stated objectives provided within the Defense Program Guidance (DPG). The DoD Program Review Group (PRG) closely scrutinizes high-priority requirements and objectives and develops resource and program issues during the OSD issue cycle, which the Defense Resources Board (DRB) subsequently reviews. The DRB recommends issue decisions to the Secretary of Defense. The senior staff in OSD and JS, plus the CINCs, judge how well the Army POM responded to the established objectives and requirements in the Defense Planning Guidance (DPG), the National Military Strategy (NMS), the CJCS's Program Recommendations, and CINC Integrated Priority Lists (IPLs). These views often shape the debate of the issue cycle and decisions. These decisions are announced in the form of Program

Decision Memorandums (PDMs), which provide direct feedback on the resourcing of high-priority programs and ultimately establish the total obligation authority (TOA) allocated each service, and more specifically the Army's portion of the DoD budget.

Internal evaluation of the Army POM considers the effects on the allocation of Army resources after the PDM is compared to the POM. However, the barometer in measuring overall success of the POM has normally been the measure of Army TOA in the POM versus the Army TOA after the PDMs. An increase in TOA for the Army usually signals a successful programming phase. However, the specific outcomes of key issues and the allocation of resources to major programs may cloud the comparative measure of TOA; in some cases where overall TOA has been increased, these individual outcomes may cause the ARSTAF to judge the programming phase to be less successful. However, prior to 1995, the Army seldom established in TAP or the APGM objective measures which could be used to evaluate the outcome of their programming efforts.

Some Major Criticisms of the POM: 1993–1995

Constraints on total resources notwithstanding, the general consensus of judgments, both internal and external to the Army, is that the FY92–97 and FY94–99 Army POMs did not adequately resource many established objectives and that resource allocation was not balanced across several competing high-priority requirements. For example, the investment area had been under-resourced since POM FY92–97 and throughout successive FYDP periods through 1995. While readiness and force structure (through resourcing of end-strength) had received the highest resource priorities for these same program cycles, several programs had been allocated insufficient resources. These included the Base Realignment and Closure (BRAC) program, with underestimated implementation costs and overestimated savings; military construction and housing; operations and maintenance functions, such as barracks modernization and depot maintenance; modernization programs, including technology development and equipment recapitalization; and more recently, active Army personnel support operations, including incentives and promotions. During the same period, the lack of Army resources to support requirements in CINC IPLs had been another cause of program criticism.

OSD and the JS have also raised significant issues with the Army concerning its resource allocation decisions. They suggested that the active Army force structure was too large, that the ratio of Army combat to the combat support (CS) and combat service support (CSS) structure was not in balance with the needs of the military strategy, and that the Army National Guard force structure was not based upon validated force requirements. They further suggested that these issues were the principal foundation for the Army's resource shortage and program imbalance problems.

As a counter to some of this criticism, the Army has argued that the program imbalance was caused by a lack of TOA coupled with priorities directed in the DPG. Further, the Army has strongly defended both the size and composition of its force structure without regard to its related high cost. The Army maintains that OSD has not allocated sufficient resources to achieve assigned program objectives and that reallocation of TOA within DoD is the key to solving its many identified program problems.

Review of these past criticisms and related arguments provided the initial basis for the project team to suggest ways to improve the programming process by developing specific measurable program objectives that were supportive of external needs, such as operational capabilities, or derived demands from the Army's statutory functions.

PROGRAMMING PROBLEMS AND ISSUES

Review and analysis of the Army programming organization and process has revealed some issues that should be addressed when considering any future improvements. Our observations were based upon interviews with senior members of the Army Secretariat and ARSTAF, JS, and OSD with recent program or resource experience. Some of these observations deal with internal perspectives of needed programming improvements, and others are externally suggested from experience with Army program outputs and OSD issue cycles.

Lack of Visibility and Participation in Programmatic Decisions

We mentioned previously that in 1995, the Army made some changes in the program review hierarchy. Those organizational changes were in response to criticism which cited the lack of participation from within the Army Secretariat. The ARB, and later the ARBSG, were designed to improve Army Secretariat involvement and increase civilian control of the PPBES and, more specifically, the program phase. The MACOMs have also voiced criticism over lack of participation in the program decision forums. A response to improve the latter was to focus the agenda of the annual Winter Senior Commanders' Conference on key issues in the program phase and to expand the information included in the MACOM POM submissions. While these improvements have been generally well received, they have not eliminated the basis for continuing criticism.

Another persistent criticism was the lack of visibility of programming choices, i.e., decisions, at the various levels of the program hierarchy and throughout the process. Usually, this criticism stemmed from lack of knowledge of specific resource changes at the detailed MDEP level and an absence of discussion, review, or debate in the formal organs for programming. This criticism was often voiced by members of the PBC, who are charged with review responsibilities and PEG oversight. As a result, the PROBE database was improved and made available to the entire ARSTAF and the Secretariat through an unclassified Army headquarters local area network to increase accessibility to the resourcing decisions. The creation of the ARB and ARBSG has caused other players to become involved and has required more senior headquarters executives to be informed on program requirements and resource-allocation activities. However, few executives with program responsibility had the time or inclination to use this tool. Lastly, the fourteen PEGs that initiated the resource allocation process in the programming phase continued to be the almost exclusive domain of the uniformed military members of the ARSTAF. The result was that increased visibility of decisionmaking remained elusive.

Program Oriented on Meeting Internal Army Objectives

The external DoD community found that the Army programming process was internally focused and did not have outputs linked to the requirements of the joint warfighting environment and to the national security goals. Army presentations often cited the DPG as the basis of their resource objectives but offered little rationale as to how programs met OSD and CINC needs. Further, it was apparent to many that the Army provided little specific guidance on support for the combatant commands at the initiation of programming and often measured its support for CINC IPLs at the conclusion of the resource process. This suggested that joint warfighting needs and issues were not objectively resourced in Army programming, a contention that raised concern at the highest levels in DoD as to the importance the Army assigned to supporting the combatant commands. Further, most program presentations provided by the Army within OSD and the JS were criticized for the lack of program rationale linked to these external needs.

Subjective Overall Program Evaluation

Both internally and externally, most people involved in resource and program activities believed Army programs through 1995 lacked balance and gave inordinate priority to retaining military force structure (and related end-strength), that the investment area had long been sacrificed to support readiness and quality of life programs, and that TOA had been allocated to programs that were both costly and inefficient—e.g., infrastructure costs lacked detailed visibility, and the operational impact of changes in resourcing was not evident. Explicit measures of TOA and issue decisions aside, the overall evaluation of the Army POM was largely subjective. Our purpose was not to grade specifics of this process but merely to identify generic problems and their solutions that may help improve the programming organization and process. From these general internal and external statements on program output, there appeared sufficient motivation for improvement.

PROJECT OVERVIEW

In early 1995, the DPA&E asked the RAND Arroyo Center to help the Army improve its ability to present and justify its resources. Members of OSD and the JS criticized the Army for not being sufficiently responsive to the current DoD environment. They argued that the Army was identifying and justifying resources only internally, rather than within a joint context and based on the current fiscal realities.[10]

The DPA&E asked the Arroyo Center project team to devise a framework and methodology for developing the Army POM 98-03 that would accomplish three main goals:

1. Help the Army PA&E respond to the issues the Secretariat had raised concerning the Army POM-development process, the number of MDEPs, and their linkage to Army resource decisions.

2. Provide visible linkage between the MDEPs and Army resource decisionmaking. Ensure that the proposed framework will help the Army develop resource options and make tradeoffs. The framework must link all resources to decisions.

3. Ensure that any proposed improvements can be implemented for POM 98-03.

The Arroyo Center indicated that a new, comprehensive framework should address the resource process concerns of the Army, OSD, and the JS already discussed. The framework had to consider such critical issues as jointness and the integration of the service staff to link the Secretariat into the resourcing process (a recommendation made in the final report of the Commission on Roles and Missions of the Armed Forces [CORM]) (CORM, 1995, pp. 4-23 and 4-24). The framework also had to tie to the current Army PPBES organizational streamlining initiatives such as the Army headquarters redesign efforts.[11] The framework needed to ensure that the Army program was

---

[10]This viewpoint is based on a series of Arroyo Center interviews in late 1994 and early 1995 with members of the OSD and JS concerning the Army's program and its ability to justify its resource decisions.

[11]In response to the CORM's recommendations, the Army conducted an 18-month analysis of alternative organizational structures for the Army headquarters. The final recommendations were provided in the Ottstott Report in early 1997.

balanced, i.e., the Army's priority demands had to be identified and resourced through an objective-based allocation of its supply of available resources, albeit constrained. Any proposed framework and process would have to be incrementally implemented because of the difficulty of fully implementing an entirely new organizational structure and process in POM 98-03.

ORGANIZATION OF THIS REPORT

Chapter Two presents the new framework and process, and Chapter Three discusses the implementation of an interim framework. Chapter Four outlines the lessons learned and the next steps. There are three appendixes: Appendix A describes the former Army programming organization and structure. Appendix B discusses the foundational strategy-to-tasks resource management (STRM), which is the basis for the Objectives-Based Planning Resource Management framework (OBPRM). Finally, Appendix C provides an example of the briefing formats that the functional PEGs used to report their resource allocations to the PBC.

Chapter Two

THE NEW FRAMEWORK AND PROCESS

This primary project activity focused on identifying a framework and a supporting process that would enable the Army to identify its resource objectives, requirements, and priorities in such a way as to develop a fiscally constrained program that was responsive to OSD and JS guidance and issues (top-down developed by leadership and given to the Army). Additionally, the framework and supporting process would support the Army's vision, institutional goals, and critical programs (bottom-up developed by the MACOMs, functionals, and staff and passed up to the Army leadership).

We developed several essential criteria for the proposed framework.

- *The framework had to be both top down and bottom up.* For instance, resource choices could be audited from the highest level—DPG or national security objectives—and resource decisions could be audited up the chain, beginning at the program element level. The generation of hierarchical sets of options is inherent to the process. The options could be within a particular Title X function, such as manning or training. The leadership should also be presented options that cut across resource areas: greater equipping versus reductions in manning; reductions in equipping versus greater technology investment, long-term research and development, etc.

- *All the Army's resources had to be considered within capability packages.* For instance, the identification of the Patriot missile system as a defense against incoming Scud missiles has to include *all the associated resources*, including those needed for deployment and sustainment of the system. Capability packages, therefore, would link resources for the service's Title X functions to the total set of capabilities they are able to provide to the joint force commander. Such an approach eliminates the practice of resourcing totally within stovepipes (a single functional area) because all the resources associated with providing a capability have to be accounted for within a single package.

- *The framework also had to ensure that tradeoff analyses are performed in a disciplined and consistent manner.* Intertemporal (near-, middle-, and far-term) issues are addressed within the tradeoffs, giving the Army's program a longer time horizon than the six years associated with the DoD program. The framework, therefore, had to ensure the auditing of decisions over time. This is more than freezing the databases at particular points in time, which is the practice now.

- *The framework had to accommodate the Army's culture and enhance the Army's core capabilities.* The Army's culture is grounded in centralized decisionmaking (with some MACOM participation) and decentralized execution. Additionally, the Army is an organization that finds it easier to accept evolutionary change than sudden change. It finds it difficult to incorporate change into the organization and more acceptable to change incrementally.

For the military services, core capabilities must contain several attributes:

- To claim a core capability, a service must have the skills and expertise that provide an important national security capability.

- The skills and capabilities must create and maintain real distinctions among the services. The Army, along with the other services, must preserve and even strengthen these distinctions because that is what makes them unique. In addition, the services' skills and capabilities must be critical to the achievement of a strategic concept.

- The capabilities that a service provides must also be important in the future.

- The capabilities must be applicable across most mission scenarios, and their utility and efficiency must be demonstrable.

— Core capabilities must also enhance an organization's competitiveness in the future, i.e., a core capability must provide long-term benefits. Therefore, to own a core capability, a service must be a key player in the critical strategic decisions that affect that capability even though other services might also have interest and investment in that capability area.

The Director PA&E provided some ground rules to limit the project and to ensure the project was primarily focused on defining a new programming framework:

1. The MDEP structure was not to be altered. MDEPs would continue to account for all Army resources. Shrinking the number of MDEPs would continue as a separate activity internal to the Army. In addition, the internal structure of individual MDEPs was to be considered as adequate.

2. PROBE would remain the resource database. However, this project would address the enhancement of the Army's overall analytic tools to support PPBS activities.

3. Concepts for the resource decision architecture would be addressed. This would include joint missions, the Title X functions, and their mapping to the joint missions.

4. Processes that affect Army resource requirements would be identified and some of their shortfalls would be discussed. These would include TAP, Total Army Analysis (TAA), and the Long Range Army Modernization Plan (LRAMP). Specific recommendations for change in these areas, however, would be deferred to a later phase of work.

5. The new framework and process must support the Army's evolving Resource Campaign Strategy, an effort to develop a resource-constrained approach to program development.

NEW FRAMEWORK AND PROCESS

The research team began by developing a conceptual overview of the basic elements of a resource strategy (see Figure 2.1). The inputs to the Army's strategic vision are (top left) external guidance from OSD, the JS, and Congress and (top right) the joint missions for which the

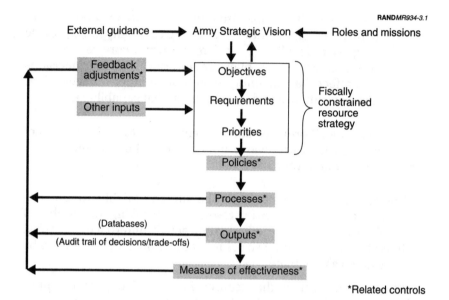

RAND*MR934-3.1*

Figure 2.1—Conceptual Overview

Army is expected to provide capabilities. This vision is the basis from which the Army defines its objectives, requirements, and priorities (center box), all of which are essential to a resource strategy. These essential elements are refined by feeding the results of policies, processes, and measures of effectiveness back into the process of defining the objectives, requirements, and priorities. The final output of this refinement process is a fiscally constrained resource strategy.[1]

The sponsor specifically requested that the recommended framework and process be consistent with and responsive to the joint environment and, in particular, the JWCA process.[2] In addition, he

---

[1]Fiscally constrained resource strategies in the military departments traditionally refer to the strategies developed by the services in response to the fiscal guidance provided to them by the OSD and the JS.

[2]The JWCA process was developed in 1995, by the then-VCJCS ADM William Owens, as a process to assess joint warfighting requirements iteratively. There are 12 JWCA areas of analysis, which are called the JWCA ribbons. These are strike; land and littoral warfare; strategic mobility and sustainability; sea, air, and space superiority; deter/counter proliferation of WMD; command and control/information warfare;

wanted the project team to build on earlier RAND work done for the Assistant Deputy Chief of Staff for Operations and Plans, Force Development (ADCSOPS-FD). We concluded that a modified application of the RAND-developed strategies-to-tasks resource management framework, the OBPRM,[3] fit the criteria. The framework was modified to allow a mapping of service issues and programs into the broader joint framework while concurrently enabling individual analysis of Army-specific issues. The backbone of the existing STRM database is a set of joint operational objectives and their associated tasks; these enable CINCs to perform joint missions. Since Goldwater-Nichols directed the services to provide the CINCs with the capabilities necessary to perform joint tasks in support of joint operational objectives, the Army needed to be able to link its activities to joint operational objectives and tasks. We concluded that the key element of the crosswalk was the identification of Army mission areas, which are broadly defined activities, specific to a particular service, that allow the joint objectives to be filtered through a service-centric perspective. The mission areas in turn are defined by major operational objectives and tasks or capabilities. The joint structure could be linked to specific service issues that were defined and debated within a joint context but in sufficient detail to ensure that all service capability issues were addressed. Figure 2.2 depicts the top-down structure, showing the crosswalk from the RAND-developed OBPRM structure to the first level of the proposed Army structure.[4]

The Army did not have a preexisting set of Army mission areas that could be directly applied. Instead, the Arroyo Center project team working with ODCSOPS derived them from several sources: The Army Modernization Plan, *The Army Focus*, POM FY94–99, and the

---

intelligence, surveillance, and reconnaissance; overseas presence; joint readiness; combating terrorism; and reengineering infrastructure. The JWCA process provides inputs into the JROC deliberations and provides the VCJCS and CJCS with information for critical decisionmaking.

[3]See Appendix B for a complete description of the STRM framework.

[4]Army mission areas are also an assessment tool for measuring how well the Army program provides its share of the joint capabilities required by the CINCs. Assessments would be focused on identifying operational capability shortfalls, deficiencies, or possible excesses. These assessments should precede the programming phase and might also be done at the completion of the POM. The former would inform the PEGs for resource allocation, while the latter assessment would identify issues not solved in the POM that could be raised to OSD in the program review cycle.

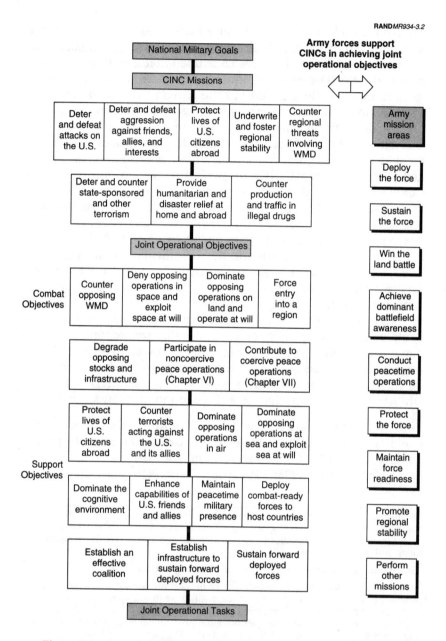

RAND*MR934-3.2*

Figure 2.2—Army Mission Areas Provide a Connection to the Joint Operational Environment

Army LRAMP. The derived list captured all of the capabilities provided by Army forces to combatant commanders in a concise, readily understood form. We then refined the list based on the previous RAND work for the JS on the integration of the JWCAs (Lewis, Schrader, Schwabe, and Brown, 1998). The Army mission areas were discussed with the sponsor prior to their modification.

The assessment of Army mission areas and associated required capabilities enabled us to define major Army resource objectives and tasks. Army-specific operational objectives and tasks allowed a particular Army mission area to be linked to the resource objectives and tasks that enabled required capabilities. They also established hierarchical measures of effectiveness because they allowed evaluation of both the Army's ability to perform and how well the task was being resourced vis-à-vis the associated objectives. Finally, one could measure the Army's ability to perform in joint mission areas through an examination of its mission areas and their ability to meet the joint operational objectives and tasks.

The proposed framework now had to be linked to an Army decision process or architecture that enabled the Army leadership to manage all Army capabilities objectively and to focus on those issues that affected the Army's performance of its organizational Title X functions. Within this framework, the mission area assessments had to inform the resource allocation process. We proposed a three-tiered decision architecture (Figure 2.3) that tied together the three major elements of the framework:

1. resource goals and objectives

2. resource subobjectives and tasks

3. MDEPs.

This hierarchy linked orthogonally to Army mission areas, major Army operational objectives, and operational tasks or capabilities.

The major issues brought before the senior leadership (top level) should focus on the ability of the Army to perform its primary functions and provide capabilities and forces in support of the National Security Strategy. The number of objectives should be small, somewhere around 20.

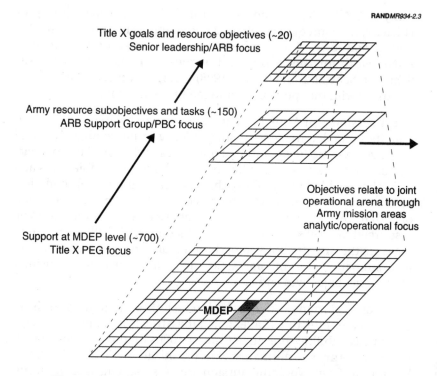

RANDMR934-2.3

Title X goals and resource objectives (~20)
Senior leadership/ARB focus

Army resource subobjectives and tasks (~150)
ARB Support Group/PBC focus

Objectives relate to joint
operational arena through
Army mission areas
analytic/operational focus

Support at MDEP level (~700)
Title X PEG focus

MDEP

Figure 2.3—Recommended Resource Decision Architecture

The second level of the decisionmaking process should concentrate on Army resource subobjectives and their associated tasks. Each subobjective and task responds to demands for capabilities and is orthogonally associated with enabling resources. It is at this level that various resourcing options and alternatives for objectives and tasks should be addressed. The ARBSG and PBC are the principal review groups involved.

The third tier (bottom level) of the hierarchy focuses on the PEGs. This provides the bottom-up efforts of the PEGs an opportunity to resource against specific resource tasks and priorities. Resulting allocations should account for all resources, including those that do not have visibility at the senior leadership or ARB level. Issues here consist of the directed activities that are resourced at the MDEP level but are not satisfied with the resources allocated to PEGs.

OBJECTIVE-BASED PROGRAMMING STRUCTURE

The second element in defining a framework and process is the linkage of the Title X functions to the Army mission areas (Figure 2.4). The Title X functions are critical because the services must perform them, as required by Goldwater-Nichols, to fulfill (to the maximum extent practicable) and enable the current and future operational requirements of the unified and specified combatant commands. The Title X functions provide the CINCs with the capabilities necessary to perform their joint operational missions. Thus, the functions must be provided to all the mission areas.

Six broad functions drawn from the 12 cited in Title X statute were identified as critical to resourcing the Army: Man, Train, Equip,

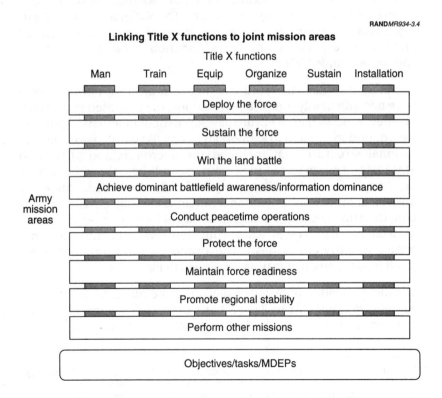

RAND*MR934-3.4*

Figure 2.4—Resource-to-Objectives Structure 1997

Organize, Sustain, and Installations.[5] In our proposed scheme, the six functions intersect with each of the Army mission areas.

The MDEPs provide a measure of how well the Army is resourcing a mission area capability; they are allocated to the PEGs based on the resource objectives and tasks that support required functions. Thus, functional decisions would then be evaluated within the mission areas. For instance, in the mission area of "deploy the force," a capability assessment would have to address the adequacy of major regional contingency (MRC) deployment assets (the metrics of adequacy have yet to be determined). These assets would be associated with specific functional tasks and their associated MDEPs. The iterative adjudication of the assignment of resources within the Army's functional responsibilities assigned to PEGs provides the mechanism by which resources would be assigned, balanced, and ultimately linked to the support of the U.S. National Security Strategy. Figure 2.5 shows the illustrative crosswalk among mission areas and the corresponding orthogonal functional resource objectives and some sample MDEPs.

As outlined earlier, the resourcing decision processes prior to 1995 were not sufficiently interactive to support the proposed framework. The new process had to ensure development of hierarchical alternatives or options. It had to support an integrated participatory organizational structure that included the Secretariat, ARSTAF, and MACOMs. The review of the resources and their allocation across the Army's Title X functional responsibilities had to link the Army mission areas to joint operational missions and objectives. In addition, the Army needed increased visibility of its total resources during its deliberative processes, which could improve its identification and review of program issues. The proposed deliberative process (bottom-up) and organization are shown in Figure 2.6.

The initial iteration of resource allocation and program issues would be done within the Army Title X PEGs (lower left of Figure 2.6) with assessment inputs from the Army Mission Areas Review Groups (on

---

[5]The original six Title X functions developed in 1995 were Man, Train, Equip, Organize, Supply, and Facilities. These were altered in 1996 by changing Supply to Sustain and Facilities to Installations to be more consistent with the broader contexts of those respective functions.

RAND*MR934-2.5*

Army mission areas	Example Army resource objectives	Related sample MDEPs	
Deploy the force	• Provide adequate deployment resources for MRCs	RJT9 RJL4 DMDE MS3J	Deployment Outload Log Over the Shore MOB Deploy Exerc Strategic Deploy.
Sustain the force	• Provide adequate war reserves	AMLC AACS VEUR ASPO	Depot Maint LCSS Conv. Ammo (SMCA) Europe Retrograde Port Operations
Win the land battle	• Provide adequate precision strike capability and munitions • Provide adequate forces for two near Sim MRCs	RF01 FPEL W582 VWR1 TCNT	Tac Bridging Apache Atk HELO 82 ABN DIV War Reserves (AR-1) National Trng Ctr
Achieve dominant battlefield awareness/ information dominance	• Provide combat IFF	GP3I FPDP FPFE FPDD WA13	NFIP/S&IA PM TENCAP PM ASAS PM JSTARS 513 MI BDE
Conduct peacetime operations	• Provide adequate training for peace operations	VMNF TCJT VLCA RJT3	Multinational Force Joint Read TNG Ctr LOG Civil Augm Prgm ASV Armored SEC VEH
Protect the force	• Provide adequate TMD capabilities	FPQC EPQF W5SD W5ND	Patriot SAM PM THAAD SWA FC ADA NATO FC ADA
Maintain force readiness	• Provide for OPTEMPO • Provide rotations to CTCs	NGBS RJL6	BOLD SHIFT ERC A Shortages
Promote regional stability	• Provide adequate peacetime HNS?	WPPM	Panama Def
Perform other missions	• Provide adequate HQDA information support systems?	FAFC PARA TACV	USA Finance Cmd RET Accural Army Civ TNG, Educ&Dev

Figure 2.5—Examples of Mapping Current MDEPs into Mission Areas and Title X Functions (PEGs) 1997

the right). The Army mission area assessments, which assessed programs versus Army mission area objectives for support of joint requirements, would be considered along with the MACOM's input. The MACOM's inputs were critical for ensuring incorporation of MACOM viewpoints on what and how capabilities could be provided into the resourcing process.

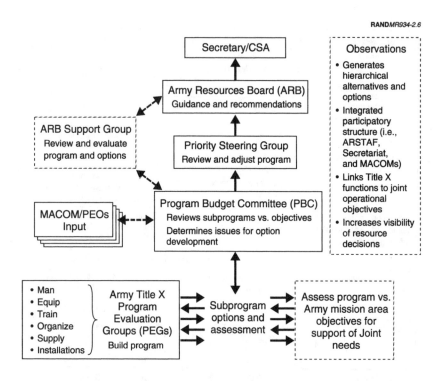

RANDMR934-2.6

Figure 2.6—1996 Program Review and Decision Structure

The interactions between the Army Title X PEGs and the Army Mission Areas Review Group were intended to result in subprogram options and assessments. For instance, an area of potential discussion could be the capabilities required for the Support Peace Operations Mission Area. Assessments of the status of these capabilities could inform the Organizing and Equipping PEGs that there are insufficient CS/CSS units and specific types of equipment to ensure the capabilities to support the joint operational objectives and tasks associated with that Army mission area. The two groups would interactively and iteratively posit several alternative ways to overcome the shortfall, with the PEGs recommending the final resource allocation.

Proposed subprograms and issues identified for future option development would be elevated to the PBC for review, integration, and higher-level cross-cutting option development. For instance, the

PBC might address the CS/CSS force structure issue by developing and proposing options that fund increases in the size of the CS/CSS and pay for it by proposing changes in the Army's operational tempo (OPTEMPO). The subprogram options and recommendations are then raised to a senior Army integrator for higher-level integration and evaluation.

The Army established an AVCSA office in September 1996 to handle some of the requirements and program integration issues within the paradigm of the ARSTAF's responsibility for requirements identification. The AVCSA's job would not be to make resource decisions but to ensure that options are developed, evaluated, and proposed to the senior Army leadership that are balanced across priority objectives and with appropriate allocations of the resources being demanded. This integration task is critical to ensuring that issues and, ultimately, the Army program are in balance—its supply (total available resources) and demand (requirements) are balanced in a manner that provides the best set of capabilities to perform the joint missions. For instance, the AVCSA might go back to the PBC with the CS/CSS-OPTEMPO option and argue that OSD guidance prohibits any reductions in the services' OPTEMPO because of near-term readiness concerns. He could ask the PBC to identify other, more-feasible options to increase the CS/CSS force; request a stronger justification for why the increases should be funded from the OPTEMPO accounts; or suggest alternative tradeoffs between unresolved issues and force structure.

The PSG is responsible for establishing priorities for major outstanding unfunded requirements and funding sources, and recommending options for solution to the ARB for review, comment, and guidance. The PSG must assure support for key operational capabilities, as well as, critical objectives related to Army functions. This interaction defines the highest tier of our three-tiered review and decision structure (Figure 2.3); it identifies the key issues that must have senior leadership review and decision because they affect the Army as an institution.

The DPA&E's guidance to the Arroyo Center project team stated that in each phase of the programming decision process members of the Secretariat were to have full participation in and visibility into the Army's resource decisions. The MACOMs were also to be given visibility. In response to this guidance, the project team recommended that the Title X review and analysis groups (PEGs) should be co-chaired by senior members of the Army staff and the Secretariat (e.g., general officers, SES staff, and deputy assistant secretaries). The organizational aspect of this recommendation was directly responsive to the guidance. This action also supported the higher purpose by providing the necessary representation to assure decisions on the allocation of the Army's resources in functional areas would support the full range of capabilities across mission areas. This requires the consideration and review of those members of the headquarters staff, both civilian and military, who are responsible for executing those decisions once they are finalized. Figure 2.7 is an illustration of how the functional program evaluation groups could be co-chaired.

SUMMARY

The new resourcing framework and process are a mechanism by which all Army capabilities are assessed and programmed. The objective is to provide a repeatable process that provides a mechanism for the Army leadership to establish priorities with clearly defined measurable objectives. The framework links to the joint arena through the Army mission areas and concurrently supports the Army's core functional responsibilities. Subsequent to the development of this approach, a foundation was laid for rebuilding Army long-range strategic planning by demanding that investment decisions be based on objectives and assessments of needed capabilities that look beyond the POM years.

The framework also integrally links Army program choices to the joint warfighting objectives and to the national security goals. In program-building activities prior to 1996, joint considerations were often incorporated into the program only after the resource choices had been determined. This approach integrates joint considerations into the process through the Army mission areas, which are derived from joint mission areas and enabled by resourcing the Army functions. Such an approach will allow the Army to build and justify its program within the context of joint missions and the CINCs.

The approach also demonstrates that the Army is a critical provider of capabilities to the joint warfighting arena. For instance, the Army provides essential capabilities to the mission areas of sustaining

RAND*MR934-2.7*

Functional Program Evaluation Groups—Example Membership

	Man	Train	Equip	Organize	Sustain	Installations
ASA(M&RA)	Ⓧ	Ⓧ		Ⓧ		
ASA(RDA)	X		Ⓧ			X
ASA(FM&C)	X	X	X	X	X	X
ASA(IL&E)	X				Ⓧ	Ⓧ
DCSOPS	X	Ⓧ	Ⓧ	Ⓧ	X	X
DCSPER	Ⓧ	X		X		
DCSLOG			X	X	Ⓧ	X
DCSINT		X	X	X		
DISC4	X		X			X
AASA				X		
ACSIM				X	X	Ⓧ
DARNG	X	X	X	X	X	X
CAR	X	X	X	X	X	X
TSG	X			X	X	X
DPAE	X	X	X	X	X	X
FORSCOM	•	•	•	•	•	•
USARPAC	•	•	•	•	•	•
EUSA	•	•	•	•	•	•
USAREUR	•	•	•	•	•	•
USARSOUTH	•	•	•	•	•	•
USASOC	•	•	•	•	•	•
TRADOC	•	•	•	•	•	•
AMC	•	•	•	•	•	•
HSC	•	•	•	•	•	•

X   Member   Ⓧ   Co-Chair   •   Participant

Figure 2.7—Title X Functional Review

forward-deployed forces and conducting peacetime operations. The Title X functions delineate the responsibilities of the services in providing capabilities and forces to joint-force commanders. In addition, the functional areas provide natural groupings by which to examine, in a balanced manner, the allocation of resources to meet the hierarchy of resource goals, objectives, and tasks.

The orthogonal linkage of functions to mission areas will enable the Army to assess the total demand against available resources. Demands for certain resources are not mutually exclusive. For instance, the demand for forces to support MRC combat and peace operations might be the same set of units; however, the training requirements for each of those demands could be significantly different and would require separate resourcing.

The proposed framework will also enhance the ability of the Army to perform hierarchical tradeoff analyses and build options in a disciplined and repeatable manner. To meet the objectives and capabilities defined within the mission areas, internal options must be developed and assessed, because the demand for resources most often exceeds the available supply, which is being heavily competed for in other mission areas. Conversely, the functional areas have only a finite amount of resources that they can provide to meet the demands across mission areas. At a higher level, the Army must decide how it will balance its resources across functional areas to meet its total resourcing obligations in all mission areas. Therefore, it might have to trade off manning resources to increase its training resources to meet increasing demands for peace operations.

The process is participatory in that the MACOMs and the Army Secretariat are involved at critical points in the decision process. The functional review groups (PEGs) are co-chaired by and composed of senior members of the Army and Secretariat staffs, thus ensuring that military judgment is linked to civilian policy perspectives and sensitivities. This integration is consistent with the intent of the Goldwater-Nichols legislation.

Chapter Three

IMPLEMENTATION OF THE NEW FRAMEWORK AND PROCESS

The DPA&E was concerned about the Army's ability to implement the new framework fully, given the POM schedule. Any change could induce some organizational and process turbulence. TAP had been approved and published in October 1995; by November, the POM process had already begun, still structured around the 14 functional PEGs. The PBC had fully institutionalized the existing PEG-MDEP structure. The existing PEG representatives had already articulated strong resistance to changing the current PEG structure or even eliminating a few marginal PEGs.

The new framework and process discussed in Chapter Two required phased implementation by the Army leadership; the Arroyo Center made modifications concerning implementation of the process in late 1995. The then-current Army POM development organization and processes could only partially support the framework and required modification. For instance, the existing PEG structure was very cumbersome and narrowly stovepiped by a combination of functional and organizational groupings that needed to be restructured according to the six broad Title X functions. Subsequent work has focused on full implementation of the framework, including the mission areas.

The process by which these PEGs allocated resources, adjudicated resource issues, and were assigned MDEPs also needed to be altered. The then-current process lacked discipline and did not explicitly identify resource objectives, set priorities, or provide an audit trail of resource decisions and tradeoffs. For example, why were certain resource demands given priority over others? What requirements had resources traded away to fund other demands?

The DPA&E, in coordination with ODCSOPS, assured TAP would be incorporated into the new process. Prior to 1996, all the MDEPs were individually assigned to one of the 14 PEGs, based on the broadly stated resource objectives found in TAP. Importantly, since each PEG prepared the objectives associated with its corresponding resource area, TAP did not explicitly identify priorities within or across the PEGs, priorities within the total Army, or measures of effectiveness. Effectiveness was most often measured by the number of MDEPs resourced without any determination of the capabilities provided the Army.

TAP was built around the existing PEG objectives rather than the capability needs recommended Army mission areas. As late as early January 1996, the mission area proponents had not been identified, and the new panels were not operational. Members of the office of the DPA&E expressed concerns over the Army's ability to formulate, prepare, and fully operate the mission area assessment panels in the time available. In addition, MDEPs had not yet been realigned according to the new Title X-six PEG organizational structure.

INTERIM PROGRAM ORGANIZATION

These concerns were sufficient to cause the DPA&E to ask for an incremental implementation of the new framework and process. An incremental implementation would allow the Army to gradually put into place key elements of the new framework and process with less turbulence at the time of the on-going programming phase. The incremental approach, however, would strongly signal to the Army staff the leadership's concern with developing a balanced program that responded to OSD's and the JS's issues and that could be justified in the budget to Congress. Further, such an approach supported other needed improvements, such as increased participation by the Army Secretariat, improved visibility of the resource-allocation process, more discipline in resource decisionmaking, and open consideration of alternative resource tradeoffs.

The most contentious area for implementation was the alteration of the current PEG structure. Many existing PEG chairs argued that realigning the MDEPs among new PEGs was institutionally too hard to do within the allowable time. Nevertheless, the DPA&E decided that the existing PEG structure and its associated MDEPs would be re-aligned according to the six broad Title X functions. Lacking the organization to assess operational objectives, capabilities, and tasks within new Army mission areas, the Mission Area Teams, the Army would program for this POM solely according to resource objectives and tasks supporting the six primary functions of the Army derived from TAP. The Army leadership would also establish and approve functional goals, objectives, and priorities for their associated resource tasks. The new PEGs would be required to allocate assigned resources according to their resource tasks and priorities and among their MDEPs.

To increase the involvement of the Army Secretariat, each new PEG would be co-chaired with a representative from the appropriate cognizant office in the Secretariat and a representative from the cognizant ARSTAF agency. For example, the training PEG is co-chaired by the Office of the Assistant Secretary of the Army (Manpower and Reserve Affairs) and the Office of the Deputy Chief of Staff for Operations and Plans (ODCSOPS). Further, the rank of these co-chairs was raised to be equivalent to general officer or SES to ensure early, continuous, and responsible senior management oversight and involvement. The full PEG membership was then enlarged to accommodate those Secretariat and ARSTAF agencies with policy, program, or execution responsibility.

PARTIAL IMPLEMENTATION OF THE NEW FRAMEWORK AND PROCESS

The partial implementation of the new framework and process required that a different set of linkages be identified before the commencement of Title X functional PEGs' deliberations. The focus was now on establishing measures of effectiveness for allocating resources within the modified resourcing stovepipes (PEGs). At some point in the process, the operational objectives and tasks associated with mission areas would have to be integrated back into the deliberations to rebalance the Army-centric perspectives and choices with those of OSD and Congress.

It was determined that a structure similar to that of OBPRM would be built, focused on adjusting PEG resource allocations. The process used to support the framework would focus on programming to resource objectives. It would also adhere to the three-tiered decision-making construct discussed in Chapter Two. The hierarchical framework would be organized according to total Army goals and resource objectives, subobjectives, and tasks. Figure 3.1 shows the partial framework, the Mission Area teams being the only element missing from full implementation.

ARMY FUNCTIONAL GOALS

The Arroyo Center team drew up an initial set of total Army functional goals, since they formed the highest level of the new resource

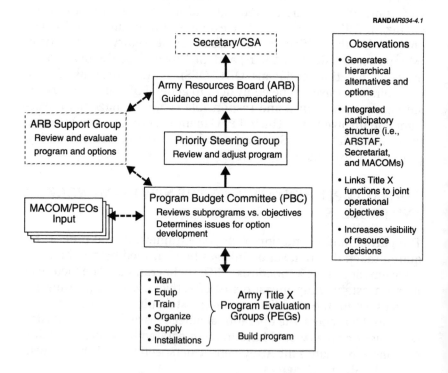

RAND*MR934-4.1*

Figure 3.1—Partial Framework

framework. Army functional goals were identified within the context of the total Army as a provider of capabilities. The goals were drawn primarily to support the 12 functions assigned the Army in Title X of the United States Code but streamlined to support the six representative functions most often noted in existing Army policy statements, Army doctrinal documents, and several recent Army publications. They were further modified to ensure that only qualitative references to resources were included.[1] ARSTAF reviewed and revised the goals, which the Army leadership ultimately approved. These goals identify the enduring values of the Army as an organization and change little over time. The following six institutional-level functional goals were identified in 1996:[2]

1. **Man**—Resource programs at levels that attract and retain sufficient high-quality personnel.

2. **Train**—Achieve directed levels of readiness to meet the needs of warfighting CINCs and execute other Title X functions.

3. **Equip**—Extend current technology overmatch into the future through modernization and recapitalization.

4. **Organize**—Provide the Total Army force structure required to achieve directed capabilities.

5. **Sustain**—Ensure sufficient support for CINC Operation Plans and other direct operational missions.

6. **Installations**—Maintain at least minimal essential infrastructure to execute Title X responsibilities.

Resource Objectives

The second level of the new resource framework is the resource objectives. The Arroyo Center project team derived the initial set from TAP and discussions with the Army leadership and staff. Resource objectives were developed for each of the goals supporting the six

---

[1]Such terms as "providing sufficient" or "maintain the minimal essential" capabilities were used to establish the baseline for the resource objectives needed to meet a goal.

[2]It should be noted that these goals were subsequently evolved with each edition of the APGM, Section III of TAP.

streamlined Title X functions. The resource objectives form the highest level of review (the top tier of the three-tiered structure). Ultimately, the resource objectives that were not adequately resourced in the program would form the key issues for leadership review and decision. ARSTAF revised the initial list of resource objectives, and Army leadership approved the final one. Seventeen resource objectives were initially identified across the six PEGs (functions). The 1996 resource objectives are listed in Table 3.1.

Table 3.1

1996 Army Resource Objectives

Function	Number	Resource Objective
Man	1.1	Maintain an affordable end strength of no more than 495,000 AC, 575,000 RC, and civilian manpower to support the required warfighting force and to meet essential force sustainment functions
	1.2	Provide for special programs and quality-of-life initiatives that contribute to Total Army Readiness
Train	2.1	Provide for DPG-specified force elements at directed levels of readiness at reduced costs by investing in modern training technologies
	2.2	Provide for officer acquisition, initial entry, leader development, and other training and education programs that link critical individual skills to unit skills by reducing: man days; temporary duty status; permanent change of station; trainees, transients, holdees, and students infrastructure; and manpower costs by investing in training technology
	2.3	Provide the Army for a continental U.S.-based power projection capability
	2.4	Ensure that Army's military operations support the national military strategy across the full spectrum of conflict
Equip	3.1	Efficiently support the requirement of the Army Modernization Program and Plan to meet joint warfighting requirements
	3.2	Provide for resource-efficient research, development, and acquisition infrastructure required to support essential science and technology, and test and evaluation and munitions management
	3.3	Invest in the Total Army standard for Horizontal Technology Integration of digitization, automation, and information management to improve resource efficiency

Table 3.1—continued

Function	Number	Resource Objective
Organize	4.1	Establish MTOE force structure and TDA direct support forces to meet wartime requirements of the NMS as articulated in DPG Illustrative Planning Scenarios
	4.2	Provide minimum essential table of distribution and allowances structure to provide peacetime sustainment and training and wartime mobilization and power projection capabilities for the Army modified table of organization and equipment force structure
	4.3	Support programs that serve special needs of the Total Army
	4.4	Provide the necessary civilian workforce to implement the Army's portion of the NMS
Sustain	5.1	Provide affordable investment in core logistics programs that support Army warfighting capability and the Army Strategic Logistics Plan as it develops, integrates, and fields initiatives vital to improvements in logistics effectiveness and efficiency
	5.2	Provide essential Army War Reserve capability to support warfighting needs
Installations	6.1	Provide an efficient base operations support program that ensures essential services and facilities to support readiness of the force at the same standard for all Army installations
	6.2	Invest in barracks, family housing, and other critical facility programs to achieve standards on an affordable schedule

The Army resource framework objectives specify both qualitative and quantitative measures. For instance, a qualitative subobjective in the manning function for objective 1.2 was "restore investment in barracks, housing and facility revitalization to achieve established standards and schedule," while in the training function, a quantitative measure was assure "'X' force elements at 'Y' level of readiness (per DPG)."[3] Seventeen resource objectives were identified across the six functions.

---

[3]Of course, we have used the generic "X" and "Y" values to substitute for the classified values provided in the actual APGM.

Resource Subobjectives and Tasks

Once the Army resource objectives were approved, resource sub-objectives and tasks were developed. These were also derived from TAP and staff knowledge of capability needs. A subobjective amplifies and disaggregates a resource objective into component elements. It provides a mechanism to gain greater functional specificity of an objective and ensure fidelity of associated tasks. A resource task is the lowest level of resource guidance and is an enabler of the resource objectives and subobjectives. The ARSTAF developed the resource tasks and recommended priorities to the Army leadership for approval. For POM 98-03, 187 resource tasks were approved, allocated to the appropriate PEGs, and assigned priorities.

Priorities for Resource Tasks

Resource task priorities were developed to ensure that the PEGs would have sufficient guidance to support their allocation of resources. The priorities consider, at the highest level, the *relative* importance across all functions of the Army, and at other levels, the *relative* importance within a specific functional area or PEG. The priorities are in four hierarchical groupings but were not directly related to specific resourcing levels (i.e., there are no established minimum amounts or percentages of funding required by a priority, and priorities do not direct a specific hierarchy of resources). These priorities also address the criticality and associated risk of an activity *relative* to other activities. The risk to the achievement of Army goals and resource objectives is also a direct consideration within these priorities, with higher priorities having little margin for risk and lower priorities having the potential to assume increased risk. Once again, risk should not be directly associated with resource levels. For instance, a Priority III task could be resourced fully, since partial resourcing might produce excessive risk (e.g., breach a contract threshold). The priorities used for the Army POM in the Spring of 1996 are shown below:

- **Priority I:** These tasks are of fundamental importance to the overall achievement of the specified goals of the Army as an institution (*not* the individual components or commands within the Army, such as the Training and Doctrine Command [TRADOC]).

They have major influence on the Army's role of providing for the operational needs of the CINCs. The tasks are generally enduring, and their achievement is directly related to the objectives of the NMS. Tasks assigned this priority are the most important to the Army leadership, and very little risk to their achievement should be accepted.

- **Priority II:** These tasks are important to the achievement of the key resource objectives within a primary function of the Army (Man, Equip, Train, etc.). They either broadly or directly support the principal elements of their related function and are considered critical to its achievement over the long term. There should be low risk associated with the achievement of these tasks.

- **Priority III:** These tasks are important to enabling some portion or subsystem of a primary function of the Army. They are supportive of narrow aspects of resource objectives. Their achievement usually supports or enables a key resource subobjective of that function. There should be no more than moderate risk associated with the achievement of these tasks.

- **Priority IV:** These tasks are of lesser importance (i.e., not Priorities I–III) and require either program visibility (i.e., in response to Army, OSD, CINC, or congressional special interest or directed guidance), close coordination among more than one PEG, or exchange of resource information among one or more staff agencies and MACOMs.[4] They can be related to one or more primary functions of the Army or a number of key resource objectives. Generally, these tasks do not pose any significant risk to the achievement of the overall Army goals or key resource objectives.

Resource Allocation Process

The six functional PEGs were also assigned a process framework and a schedule of events to guide their resource deliberations and decisions. Data were provided to the PEGs to establish a baseline for

---

[4]It should be noted that the Priority IV tasks have subsequently been replaced by Priority 0 tasks that require multiple PEG coordination or special visibility and are not ranked according to their strict resource priority (i.e., Priority I– II).

their assigned MDEPs based upon the recent Army budget and FYDP, new unprogrammed requirements and requested adjustments, and information on MACOM programmatic decisions. The PEGs reviewed and validated the many requirements supporting their assigned resource tasks and MDEPs. Using their specified resource objectives and tasks, along with stated priorities, the PEGs were provided a structure for allocating resources within their functions. Next, DPA&E allocated Army program resources to the six PEGs. A schedule for resource-allocation decisions, data outputs, and related PBC briefings from the PEGs was then established. Together, these provided the PEGs a structured process for producing functional subprograms for review, adjustment, and integration that are the foundation of the Army POM. Other levels of review and adjustment, such as the ARB, ensured program balance and issue resolution in progress to a final program review and approval by the Army leadership.

A TRANSPARENT AND DISCIPLINED PROGRAMMING PROCESS

The DPA&E also required mechanisms to ensure that the resource allocations of the PEGs were both transparent and disciplined. To support this requirement, an interactive spreadsheet connected to relational databases that contained the resource objectives and tasks (already covered) and the joint operational missions, objectives, and tasks was developed (see Appendix B). These spreadsheets guided the PEGs in developing and providing information on their review of requirements, deliberations on alternative ways to meet assigned tasks, and later their resource-allocation decisions among tasks and MDEPs. The information the PEGs provided in these spreadsheets allowed the establishment of a baseline for requirements prior to any decisions on allocation of resources. Later spreadsheet information documented the PEG resource-allocation considerations, tradeoffs, and decisions. Comparison of these sets of PEG information provides an audit trail for review by both the PBC and elements in DPA&E that are responsible for reviewing these resourcing decisions in relation to the operational needs of Army mission areas.

The PEGs were also asked to assess their allocation of the resources assigned to them. An assessment scale was devised to score each resource task. The assessments were included with other information entered in the spreadsheets corresponding to the decisions supporting PROBE data inputs for POM File 1.0. In addition to the assessments, resource tasks that were not changed from the original resource baseline (PROBE Base File 3.0)[5] were listed as **No Change.**[6] The three possible assessment scores are as follows:

- **A:** *Adequately* resourced to ensure all validated requirements so this task can be accomplished.

- **P:** *Partially* resourced but will not accomplish all validated requirements of this task.

- **U:** *Unfunded* and validated requirements of this task will not be accomplished.

Use of relational databases allowed the review and analysis of resource allocations to individual resource tasks, allocations to the tasks that support each subobjective, and allocations that support each of the resource objectives in each of the functional areas. This allowed visibility of resourcing decisions versus assigned priorities and knowledge of tradeoffs made from the baseline. The data also supported the development of alternative funding sources for selected resource issues. Further, this information allowed application of the initial OBPRM architecture to consider resourcing adjustments, with the assistance of the PEGs, to improve support for joint operational needs during the PBC's deliberations.

Common information briefing formats were also developed (see Appendix C) and provided to the PEGs for presentation of their resource decisions to the PBC. These formats focused on assessments of resourcing at the objective level, summarized assessments of tasks within priority groupings (A, P, and U), identified resource issues,

---

[5]This was the situation in the spring of 1996, but it should be noted that the number of Base Files and POM Files is often unique to the specific programming year. Additional data files are used as needed, in particular, some POM Files have recorded intermediate decision points of the PSG and ARB.

[6]PROBE database positions during Army programming fall into two categories. Base Files record current resource positions and new requirements, usually from the MACOMs. POM Files iteratively record new resource-allocation decisions until the creation of POM File 3.0 (or the appropriate number), which records the final program decisions of the Secretary of the Army and the CSA.

and made an overall assessment of the capability to accomplish the function in both the near and far terms (budget years and program years, respectively). Use of common presentations allows the PBC to identify cross-cutting issues, to determine potential sources for issue resolution, and to develop a sense of the program balance across the six functions. Subsequently, the PBC can issue guidance to the PEGs to make resource allocation adjustments that will address many of the identified but unresolved resource issues.

MISSION-AREA OPERATIONAL CONSIDERATIONS

During the program development process in 1996, the outputs of these six PEGs—both initial validation of requirements and resource allocation decisions-were assessed within DPA&E against joint operational requirements using the new mission areas and their associated joint operational objectives and tasks. These assessments provided a cross-cutting examination of how Army resource decisions addressed joint and OSD needs, including those identified by the CINC IPLs. The DPA&E recommended appropriate alternative resource adjustments to enable key operational needs to the PBC for consideration and direction to the PEGs for execution. This operational assessment, albeit limited by the knowledge and experience of PA&E personnel, was accomplished concurrently with the PEG briefings of their POM File 1.0 decisions to allow timely discussion and direction to the PEGs for inclusion in POM File 2.0 resource adjustments.

Mission Area assessments were then reviewed, adjusted, and presented to each subsequent resource review body (e.g., PSG) to provide information on outstanding operational issues and the overall level of support the Army program provided to address joint operational needs. This ensured that resource decisionmakers understood how their resource decisions affected joint operational objectives and tasks during their reviews. While the Mission Area assessments were limited in depth, they were provided a basis for adjusting resource-allocation decisions. However, these assessments did not provide the necessary foundation for the resource allocation as they were developed and accomplished in-process. While they ensured that joint operational needs received increased visibility and direct consideration during the Army's programming process, the need to begin earlier in the process with dedicated Mission Area teams was recognized in subsequent full process implementation.

The analytic utilization of the new mission areas during the 1996 review of the PEG resource decisions, however, became a concern to members of the PA&E staff. They concluded that because the mission areas had not been sufficiently vetted within the ARSTAF, their use for adjudication of resources would not be valued and could contribute to unnecessary debate within the ARSTAF that detracted from the POM process. They favored reliance on the IPLs as the final basis for assessing PEG decisions in meeting CINC requirements. The Arroyo Center project team maintained that such an approach looked retrospectively at resource decisions and identified where they coincidentally satisfied IPL requirements. As a result, these decisions did not significantly weigh long-term CINC needs, but rather focused on near-term resource needs. The project team also reasoned that the approach was not significantly different from how the Army had previously evaluated its resource decisions in the joint arena.

The DPA&E subsequently concluded that the mission areas should be used for internal assessments of how the PEG decisions met joint requirements. He also wanted the mission areas to provide some indication of where any remaining funds should be allocated, providing only marginal utility to these assessments. In addition, there were a number of areas that the DPA&E felt were overresourced and from which some funding could be reallocated to those areas that were not sufficiently resourced. However, he wanted these decisions based on some qualitative and (if available) quantitative analysis.

Several action officers from PA&E, with the support of the Arroyo Center project team, performed the operational assessment. The evaluation was designed around the tasks associated with each of the mission areas, the demands identified in the CINCs' IPLs, and the allocation of resources within the PEGs based on the agreed-upon resource goals, objectives, and tasks. The assessment focused on both the number of times a single issue was raised in the IPLs and its association with the tasks contained in the mission areas. For example, several of the warfighting CINCs raised the issue of sufficient CS/CSS units to support both their MRC requirements (modeled and supported by the Army) and their ongoing peacetime mission activities (not separately resourced by the Army). The need for the Army to provide sufficient numbers of CS/CSS units appeared many times in the IPLs. The combination of the requirements for CS/CSS for the Army to perform certain tasks associated with several mission areas and the need the CINCs articulated vis-à-vis the IPLs enabled the assessment team to determine that the demand for CS/CSS units and equipment was quite high.[7] This qualitative assessment was provided to the Army to assist in the final adjudication of resources and to help ensure that a balanced POM was developed.

---

[7]Bottom-Up Review guidance indicated that Army peacetime requirements should be met with the resources for wartime missions.

Chapter Four

LESSONS LEARNED AND NEXT STEPS

The evaluation of the new POM process was completed in two parts. First, the DPA&E directed that an after-action, lessons-learned activity be conducted to assess what needed to be changed and improved upon for the next POM. In early July 1996, the PEG executives and administrators from across the ARSTAF, as well as, representatives from Director of Information Systems for Command, Control, Communications, and Computers (DISC4); the National Guard Bureau (NGB); Office, Chief of Army Reserve (OCAR); and the Army Budget Office (ABO) met to discuss their views and make recommendations on how the newly implemented process might be further improved. Second, the Arroyo Center project team conducted its own interviews with several key participants from the offices listed above and from offices within DCSOPS, DPA&E, and AVCSA, who represented various perspectives on the revised process.[1]

Generally, the participants in the revised POM process agreed that the Army had needed to change its process and realign it to better reflect the current resource environment. Few participants had problems with the new framework, although it was clear from the project team interviews that most of the participants viewed the new process as being a reconfiguration of the PEGs along the six stream-

---

[1]The 1996 POM FY98-03 After-Action Review (AAR) is contained in a memorandum for distribution dated July 18, 1996, from the Chief of the PA&E Program Development Division. The Arroyo Center conducted interviews with members of the ARSTAF and participants in the POM process from July to August 1996. Individuals were interviewed from the DCSOPS, Installation, and Modernization and Force Development directorates.

lined Title X functions and the development of resource objectives and tasks. However due to the limited involvement during the POM with Mission Area assessments, few knew about or understood the intended role of the mission areas in the revised process. Most agreed that the resource goals, objectives, and tasks enabled them to assess how well they did in allocating available resources within their new PEG structures. The Army National Guard and Army Reserve participants viewed themselves as having done well in the process and indicated that sharing their resource concerns within the context of the total Army enabled them to better articulate their resource needs. Many of the Reserve Component resource requirements were assessed as adequately funded.

Some general criticisms of the framework and process used during the 98-03 POM emerged:

- Limited audit trail of decisions and challenges to perceived organizational prerogatives

- Lack of consistency across the PEGs in terms of resource objectives and tasks

- Problems with the assignment of the MDEPs to the PEGs

- Army's compressed POM schedule

- Questionable future relevancy of TAP and the APGM

- Need for more participation of the Secretariat and MACOMs

- Problems with coordination.

The Arroyo Center project team developed the following recommendations for improving the partially implemented framework and process based upon our involvement in the process, in depth staff interviews, and review of the criticisms:

- Align MDEPs with PEGs based on resource capability packages

- Alleviate the pressures of a compressed Army POM schedule by maintaining an Army resource process throughout the year

- Refocus and revise TAP and the APGM so that they are more strongly linked[2]

- Increase MACOM participation in debates on alternatives and options during PEG meetings

- Encourage more active Secretariat participation in their role as PEG co-chairs while ensuring that PEG guidance meetings and co-chair meetings are used to address concerns and the cross-cutting issues rather than recreating old stovepipes

- Develop a single resource database and analytic tool architecture that enables the planning process to link the programming activities and the programming function to map to the budgeting function

- Redesign TAP to incorporate Army mission areas to provide the capacity to measure the Army's ability to perform the tasks and provide capabilities associated with the mission areas.[3]

LIMITED AUDIT TRAIL

Many participants in Army POM 98-03 were divided on the ability of the process to ensure that decisions were audited. Some argued that the revised framework enabled them to measure iteratively how well they were allocating their resources to meet objectives and tasks. They were able to perform "what if" drills and trade-off analyses within their respective PEGs. This approach enabled them to better defend their decisions within the review bodies and to garner more resources. Others argued that the framework and process challenged their traditional modes of operation. The process forced them to disaggregate single, large MDEPs containing billions of dollars to demonstrate how they were meeting their respective resource objectives and tasks. They felt that the process challenged their organiza-

---

[2]This recommendation recognized that ODCSOPS had already published TAP prior to the development and implementation of the new process along with the expanded APGM, which established the resource goals, objectives, subobjectives, and tasks and their related priorities. A more conventional ordering of guidance was intended and needed for future program iterations. ODCSOPS agreed with this recommendation.

[3]ODCSOPS also agreed for the need to assure that long-range strategic planning was accomplished to provide specific near-, mid-, and long-term guidance and objectives in TAP to the Mission Area Teams and PEGs.

tional prerogatives. Some argued that several PEGs did not "play the game" fairly, in that they refused to show how they allocated their resources across the objectives and tasks of their respective PEGs. However, many PBC members applauded the increase in visibility of the resource allocation done by the PEGs.

LACK OF CONSISTENCY ACROSS THE PEGs IN TERMS OF RESOURCE OBJECTIVES AND TASKS

Many interviewees contended that the resource objectives and tasks were internally consistent within a functional area but were not at a consistent level across the PEGs. Therefore, the total resourcing of the Army could not be evaluated because of the lack of uniform standards and measures. The DPA&E had anticipated this problem prior to the partial implementation of the new framework.

In part, this is attributable to the allocation of resources (MDEPs) within the six new functional areas. In the fully implemented framework, the integration function would be the iterative assessment of the Army's ability to support the various capability needs found in the Army Mission Areas.

INADEQUATE LINKAGE OF THE MDEPs TO THE FUNCTIONAL AREAS

The MDEP alignment according to the functional areas (PEGs) was another concern raised by several interviewees. They contended that many MDEPs did not completely align with the six functional areas. Instead, elements were distributed across several functional areas. Some PEG chairs found this to be confusing and believed that it limited their ability to make resource decisions. Some PEGs, such as sustainment, had no MDEPs in specific areas of their interest and felt obligated to hand off their resource recommendations to a number of other PEGs.

This difficulty is attributable to problems with the MDEP structure extant in 1996 and selected Army practices. The first was the deviation of the MDEP structure from its original design, focused on resource capability packages, to a focus on appropriation categories. The next problem was the Army's concentration on resourcing individual items down to appropriation level through the prior 14 PEGs, who believed that they "owned" the resources found in the MDEPs. Further, some PEG chairpersons were preoccupied with the construct that to resource a function, they had to own the associated MDEPs, rather than viewing MDEPs as categories that account for resources after the resources have been allocated to programs.

The project team also identified two structural problems: First, a small number of resource objectives contained billions of dollars that literally covered the entirety of a PEG's function and resources. For instance, the equipping PEG had one resource objective that contained all the funding for Army modernization. The amount of resources and large number of MDEPs associated with this single resource objective prevented the equipping PEG from robustly debating the allocation of its resources based on the existing needs with equipping. The second problem was that some MDEPs contained such a large amount of resources as to conceal the allocation of resources to specific objectives and tasks. For instance, within the manning PEG, a single MDEP covering the pay, allowances, PCS travel, and bonuses for active military amounted to over $20 billion per year. This failed to provide the necessary transparency for the appropriate review bodies, such as the PBC, to determine the actual adequacy of funding for several included programs. These problems resulted in several sessions in which the ARB and Army leadership asked the PEG co-chairs to provide better justification for their choices rather than relying on a description of how much funding a particular MDEP had received.

THE ARMY'S COMPRESSED POM SCHEDULE

The participants in the process were unanimous in their criticism of the POM-development timeline. Some of these problems were internal to the Army; others arose because OSD was slow to provide critical documentation, such as the Defense Planning Guidance (DPG) and fiscal guidance. The POM process began late, and then, in early December 1995, the Army leadership approved changing the process. As a result, much of the staff was rushed, and many felt that some critical issues were not thoroughly coordinated. Several problems were not resolved until quite late in the process.

We observed that many of these frustrations could be eased if the Army maintained a resource process throughout the year. The POM process within the Army is responsive to OSD guidance and schedule, and the Army leadership recognizes that resource requirements and allocation are a main activity of a service headquarters. However, the development of key documents that provide resource guidance across the Army is integral to the implementation of a total resourcing framework and process. Similar problems had been observed in the Army's difficulties in supporting the JS's JWCA. We believe that, in part, this was attributable to the Army's narrow focus on the key resource allocation, review, and decision events of the POM process during that period rather than on the broader activity of organizationally and functionally supporting year-round requirements and resources strategies.

All the services, no matter how well the process was organizationally and functionally supported, had problems meeting the OSD deadlines in the preparation and delivery of their POMs. The POM schedule has always been dominated by some glitches and last-minute decisions. The goal, therefore, is to develop a schedule that enables the staff to handle the glitches. Some Army staff members recommended that the POM-building process commence one month earlier. The Army After Action Review recommended the staff should go with the best fiscal guidance that it has at the time and then adjust its data after receiving final fiscal guidance.[4]

THE FUTURE RELEVANCY OF TAP AND THE APGM

The relevancy and linkage of TAP and APGM to the POM-development process was an issue raised by many members of the ARSTAF. Functionally, TAP described the total demand for resources as defined by various internal Army processes.[5] Traditionally, the PEGs have defined the resource requirements in TAP and then resourced them in the POM, a very parochial process. The APGM prior to 1996

---

[4]Army AAR, July 18, 1996.

[5]For instance, the Total Army Analysis (TAA) that determined the composition and structure of the Army, and which drove the active and reserve component end-strength, was one such process. The Army leadership decisions within the TAA became directed guidance in TAP.

contained the instructions for the preparation of the POM and some final resource guidance. Some participants indicated that, with the definition of Army resource objectives and tasks and the proposed changes to TAP that would reorganize it along Army Mission Areas, the APGM might also be changed to more clearly reflect changes in the resourcing process. Some even suggested that the APGM should be merged with TAP and that TAP should become the integrating mechanism for the overall POM process.[6]

We concurred that both documents need refocusing and revision that would link them more strongly. TAP should both establish the demand for Army resources vis-à-vis the Mission Areas and shape the institutional demand. It should also provide an integration mechanism through its linkage to the functional areas (PEGs). The Army could then evaluate how well the functional areas have allocated their resources in support of the mission areas and their associated objectives and tasks. In this schema, the DPA&E maintains responsibility for integrating the functional areas in addition to the larger activity of balancing total resources against total demand vis-à-vis the APGM.

The APGM is a guidance document that defines what objectives and capabilities the POM is expected to yield. It sets the programming priorities. It should identify the priorities being placed on the institutional objectives, the measurement criteria and standards for them, the identification of all available resources, and the initial division among the competing functional areas. It should also update the schedule of events and any changes to desired outputs. It could also become a portion of TAP but would need to be timed in publication to be germane to the programming phase.

NEED FOR GREATER PARTICIPATION OF THE SECRETARIAT AND MACOMS

Some of the participants argued that given the time schedule for the POM and the introduction of the new process, the process was not as

---

[6]Subsequent to this research the APGM was configured to be Section III of TAP and performed the recurring function for which it was first used during POM 98-03 of establishing resource goals, objectives, tasks, and their related priorities.

participatory as it should have been. They also noted that the process relied on the resident knowledge of the former PEG chairpersons who had overseen the original 14 PEGs. The lack of timely guidance from the DPA&E and ODCSOPS to the new Title X PEG executives and/or administrators resulted in the ARSTAF PEG co-chairs disseminating critical information which placed the Secretariat co-chairs in a dependent role. The ARSTAF PEG co-chairs, through their participation in Resource Battle Staff meetings, resolved the cross-cutting PEG issues.[7] The AAR called for the PA&E to reestablish the regular PEG executive and/or administrator meetings, the forum in which concerns, solutions to problems, and cross-PEG issues could be raised and resolved. These meetings would assure the both PEG co-chairs were informed in a timely fashion prior to PEG resource allocation decisions.

We found that the lack of participation by the MACOMs and the Secretariat was attributable to several observed organizational and functional disconnects. Although the MACOMs were asked to participate in the headquarters process, their early POM submittals contained their resource decisions, thereby constraining their active participation in the PEGs to a "damage limiting" activity. Alternatives and options to proposed MACOM programs were debated within the MACOMs but on occasion were not shared with the MACOM representatives at the PEG meetings. MACOM representatives were sometimes unaware that agreements had been struck between the MACOMs and the PA&E staff.

The Secretariat's participation was designed into the process through the development of PEG co-chairs. Several participants from the Secretariat contended that, given the tight POM schedule, they had insufficient time to become fully knowledgeable about the issues. However, in retrospect they supported the goal of the revised process to be more inclusive and participatory and felt that the Secretariat's involvement would be stronger in the next POM iteration, given that the process was now familiar to them. They indicated that they wanted to play a greater role in the development of the resource goals, objectives, and tasks, which would provide a strong knowledge base for working in the PEGs. They did not disagree with the

---

[7]Army AAR, July 18, 1996, slide 8; Arroyo Center–conducted interviews, July 1996.

reestablishment of the regular PEG executive and/or administrator meetings, but they had some concerns about the process becoming too bogged down in coordination meetings.

We felt that the reestablishment of the PEG executive and/or administrator meetings could recreate the old stovepipe. We recommended that the guidance meetings and co-chair meetings be used to address concerns and the cross-cutting issues. This approach would be consistent with the new process and eliminate additional coordination meetings while providing improved coordination across the entire programming process.

COORDINATION

Although the issue of coordination was similar to the above-discussed issue of participation of the Secretariat and the MACOMs, sufficient differences were identified to make it a separate issue. Coordination included three key topics: (1) the timeliness of the PEGs' inputs to the DPA&E; (2) the alignment and ability of different databases used for POM development to link to one another and provide quality information for decisionmaking; and (3) the Army's ability to provide timely information to the Joint Staff and the OSD concerning their POM issues.

The most difficult problems were with the PEGs not meeting deadlines and the lack of databases that could provide sufficient detailed information. Some asserted that a few PEGs deliberately refused to meet imposed deadlines for briefing their findings, believing that they could "better play the game" by withholding information on how their decisions were reached. Other participants contended that the schedules were unreasonable and could not be met, given the added briefing requirements being demanded. We concluded that these contending perspectives were both, at least, partially accurate. Some PEGs may have deliberately missed deadlines and attempted to bypass specific review meetings; often they attempted to negotiate agreements informally. On the other hand, some PEGs struggled over hard decisions and, lacking consistent standards and measures across PEGs, could not reach clear decisions on some critical issues.

Everyone agreed, however, that current Army databases were insufficient to support the new process. Some even contended that the lack of robust databases and automated tools contributed to the sub-optimization of the process. Some of the problems identified were: (1) inconsistencies in data between the acquisition agency of the Secretariat (ASA(RDA)) and Deputy Chief of Staff for Operations and Plans–Force Development (DCSOPS-FD); (2) the inability of the PROBE database to provide in-process summaries of PEG committed resources against MDEPs;[8] and (3) the lack of access to the PROBE database to share data iteratively with the Secretariat members of the ARB. Another example was that the acquisition community provided data baselined against the President's Budget rather than according to the POM files developed by PROBE. In turn, this necessitated the rebuilding of the database once it was turned over to the equipping PEG and the DCSOPS-FD before it could be entered in PROBE.

The need to develop compatible databases and an array of analytic tools is not new to the Army; it has been a contentious point for several years. The Army would greatly benefit from a single resource database and analytic tool architecture that enables the planning process to link to the programming activities, and the programming function to crosswalk to the budgeting function. An array of analytic tools that enable the programmers and financial managers within the PEGs, DPA&E, and other agencies to develop alternatives, assess the effects of their decisions, and provide an audit trail should be embedded in the architecture. The architecture should be consistent internally, as well as with OSD and Joint Staff models. Further study is required to determine the precise requirements of this architecture of analytic tools.

IMPLEMENTATION AND NEXT STEPS

The further implementation of the OBPRM-based framework and process will occur in subsequent years. The Army was sufficiently satisfied in 1996 with the results of the partially implemented framework and process that it wants to utilize the entire framework and

---

[8]PROBE was updated for the various final POM File positions once the PEG had completed its resource allocation decisions. However, most PEG administrators had to rely on separate data bases to determine in-process summaries of resource allocation. Several participants suggested that PROBE should be modified to provide data for this PEG decision support need.

process with some modifications to the resourcing processes and alternative implementation strategies.

Soon after the Army POM 98-03 process, the Army leadership concluded that the new six PEG structure along the Title X summary functional areas was sufficient and adequate for the programming process. The future goal is to institutionalize the new framework and process. The DPA&E wants to retain the six PEGs, structure the MDEPs to better accommodate the functional PEGs and to refine the resource goals, objectives, and tasks. DPA&E requested the Arroyo Center project team to assist him in the development of a consistent set of standards and measures by which it is possible to look across all the PEGs and consistently evaluate their outputs. The DPA&E and DCSOPS also concluded that the PEGs should have ARMY Mission Area assessments of required operational capabilities as inputs to their future resource goals, objectives, and tasks.

The Chief of the Resource Analysis and Integration Office (DAMO-ZR),[9] who has responsibility for TAP, concluded that the document needed to be modified in such a way as to provide better guidance on the allocation of Army resources and their relative priorities. Since the Army had moved away from the 14 PEGs to the six Title X functional areas, he wanted to use the change as a way to restructure TAP. He asserted that TAP must be redesigned in order to be more usable and relevant to how the Army resourced itself. TAP should both provide the mechanism for identifying and setting the Army's resource priorities and become a mechanism for assessing how well the functional PEGs had done their work.

The DAMO-ZR, Arroyo Center, and the DPA&E agreed that TAP should be redesigned along the foundation of Army Mission Areas. The mission areas could provide the ability to measure the Army's ability to perform the operational tasks and provide the related operational capabilities associated with the mission areas. Because the Army mission areas were subsets of the joint mission areas, a direct link into the joint environment was established into which resources could be subsequently tied. Furthermore, the mission areas would provide the backdrop for the assessment of how well the functional

---

[9]COL H. W. Lord, Jr., discussions and interview, March and June, 1996.

panels had distributed their resources to support capability needs. Assessments could be made of both how well the resource goals, objectives, and tasks had been met within a PEG and of how well the Army provided capabilities to joint force commanders through an assessment of the Army's Mission Areas.

RAND ARROYO CENTER'S FUTURE ROLE

The Arroyo Center project team agreed to assist the Army in redesigning TAP and completing the full implementation of the new framework. The project team will help the Army further flesh out the mission areas and restructure TAP. In addition, the project team will address TAP's linkage to both the Joint Operational planning process and the Army POM process. TAP must clearly define the spectrum of demands (via the mission areas) being placed on the Army for operational capabilities and assist in balancing the allocation of resources to these demands in view of both the demands on the institution through the functional areas and the availability of resources. Therefore, TAP would define the total demand and provide a structure for integration of the supply to meet the demand. Balancing (integration) the resource allocations across the demand would foster the need for options and alternatives, thereby supporting the framework's original objective of providing visibility into the ramifications of resource choices while enabling the Army leadership to identify, review, and decide on the critical issues that most affect the current and future needs of the institution.

The development of key documents that provide resource guidance across the Army is integral to the implementation of a total resourcing framework and process. For instance, a vision document would provide some insights into what the Army leadership wants the Army to look like in the next 15 to 20 years.[10] Similarly, a long-range strategy coupled with a strategic resource plan could inform the Army on how the leadership intends to achieve the goals and objectives laid out in the vision incrementally over near-, mid-, and far-term encompassing more than the period of a normal POM cycle. The strategic resource plan could provide guidance to the functional

---

[10]As noted earlier, the Army CSA provided an Army Vision in 1996 that subsequently provided for this need.

areas in terms of the mid- to long-term priorities for certain resource areas, and it would define the standards and measures across the functional areas. An Army strategic resource plan would also provide the guidelines for the development of strategic resource plans for each of the functional areas. DPA&E requested that the Arroyo Center develop the strategic resource plan. Initial work on this commenced in the fall of 1996.

IMPLICATIONS

The full implementation of the new POM process has implications far beyond the actual POM. The new framework could provide a mechanism for how the Army defines, allocates, and manages its total resources within the Planning, Programming, and Budgeting Process (PPBS). For instance, TRADOC—the organization responsible for the development of new concepts, the writing of Army doctrine, and the design and management of Army training—could begin to define its new concepts and doctrine according to Army Mission Areas rather than its current process, which is aligned according to its branches and schools. Importantly, TRADOC's LRAMP, which provides non-fiscally-constrained modernization requirements to the ARSTAF, is currently structured around the branches' requirements, thus creating a potential disconnect between the ARSTAF, which is aligning its resources according to the demands of Army Mission Areas and the Title X functions.

The strongest impediments to the full implementation of the new framework and process are the lack of personnel stability and the lack of a cadre of trained and experienced resource managers. The constant turbulence of personnel on the ARSTAF brought on by reductions in both military and civilian headquarters personnel and the Army's rotation policies, which often transfer officers in under two years, hinders the Army's ability to sustain long-term institutional knowledge in the resource management area. The Army's focus continues to be on the training and development of field officers, generally ignoring the need for a cadre of headquarters staff officers well trained in the various resource processes within the Army, OSD, and the JS. Such a cadre could enhance the Army's ability to compete for resources. The latter difficulty can be remedied if the Army leadership identifies the strategy, planning, and resource programming functions as priority specialties and requires development of career paths that include formal and informal training in these specialties with the career incentive of advanced promotion.

The new framework and process aligns the Army much closer to the joint operational needs and the realities of the OSD and JS resourcing processes and activities. When fully implemented, these changes will give the Army the capability to assess resources within a joint operational context, evaluate their programs against the new capabilities being demanded for and fielded in the next five to ten years, and ensure that the Army's core functional competencies are sustained or modified according to changes in the strategic environment.

Since this research was conducted, the Army has initiated the reengineering of TAP in 1997. The reengineering has focused on establishing the Army Mission Areas, defining their key supporting objectives, and identifying critical capabilities that must be provided by the Army in the future.

In addition, in 1997 the Army, with the assistance of this project team, initiated development the Army Strategic Planning Guidance (ASPG), which will identify institutional and goals and objectives and operational capabilities for the near-, mid-, and long-terms. The ASPG will provide the non-fiscally-constrained institutional direction for the Army, a strategy for transforming the Army to meet the needs of the changing operational environment. This activity will strengthen the important planning phase of the Army PPBES process.

Also, Army Secretariat participation in the planning phase of Army PPBS has been enhanced through membership in the Strategy and Planning Committee (SPC) and the subordinate Strategic Planning Working Group.

Subsequent Arroyo Center projects for the Army will focus on integrating standards and measures for the PEGs and Army Mission Areas into TAP, refining the mission areas, and incorporating the ASPG initiatives. Next will be a supporting effort to institutionalize the changes in the planning and programming phases of PPBS in Army regulations.

ARMY PROGRAMMING PRE-1995

OVERVIEW

Programming is a major function within the Army's resource management and decisionmaking process: PPBES. This appendix discusses the purpose, organization, and process of the programming function during the early 1990s through 1995.[1]

THE PURPOSE OF ARMY PROGRAMMING

The purpose of Army programming is "to distribute available manpower, dollars, and materiel among competing requirements per Army resource allocation policy and priorities."[2] The programming function allocates resources to requirements that achieve the national security objectives and priorities established in the planning phases of DoD PPBS and Army PPBES. Decisions on resource allocation complete the programming phase. In addition, resource allocation decisions are the foundation of the budgeting phase, during which the needed resources are obtained from Congress.[3]

---

[1]Army Regulation 1-1: Planning, Programming, Budgeting and Execution System, January 30, 1994, p. 1.

[2]U.S. Army War College, 1995, p. 14-11.

[3]U.S. Army War College, 1995, Ch. 14.

1991–1995 ORGANIZATION OF ARMY PROGRAMMING

The programming function and related decision-making are centralized within the Army Headquarters staff but allow for inputs from MACOMs, which are the principal field operating agencies, and from PEOs, who are the materiel developers. The ASA (FM&C) provides oversight for the entire Army PPBES, with DCSOPS responsible for the planning phase along with establishing requirements and priorities, DPA&E responsible for the programming phase, and DAB responsible for the budgeting and execution phases. Several formal and informal organizations within Army Headquarters assist DPA&E in developing and reviewing program requirements, allocating resources, and helping the Army leadership make the resource decisions that result in the POM. The POM is the official documentation of Army resource decisions and is the primary input to the DoD program review and issue cycle process. We describe the organization of Army programming in the following subsections, beginning with the lowest level depicted in Figure A.1.

Management Decision Package Points of Contact

The MDEP, the official Army record for individual program information, describes the program; indicates the levels of manpower and financial resources allocated throughout the fiscal period; and identifies the staff proponent, MDEP POC, and other interested staff members.[4]

The MDEP POCs are the primary headquarters staff-level program managers and for several programs may represent the MACOMs and PEOs or Program Managers (PMs). These POCs ensure the accuracy of the MDEP information and monitor the allocation of resources to their individual programs throughout the programming, budgeting, and execution phases. They also justify program requirements, including any changes, and argue for priority in the resource allocation process. Decisions by the PEGs to allocate or change MDEP resources must be coordinated with the appropriate MDEP POC.

---

[4]AR 1-1, Section 2-12.

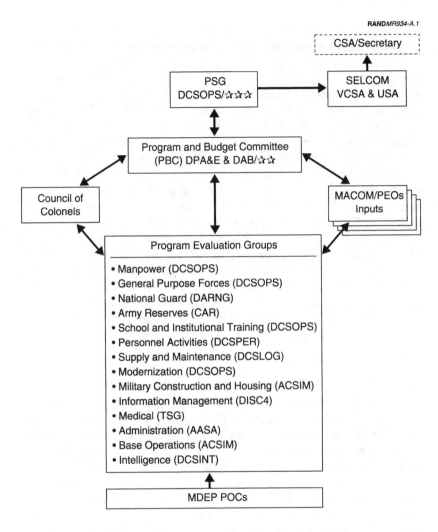

RAND*MR934-A.1*

Figure A.1—Army Resource Hierarchy Pre-1995

Program Evaluation Groups

The PEGs are the lowest organizational level in the hierarchy at the Army Headquarters involved in programming. Through 1995, the Army had 14 PEGs organized along a combination of staff functions, responsibilities, and major programs (See Figure A.1). The PEGs validate requirements, interpret resource guidance and priorities, and allocate assigned resources among assigned MDEPs. PEG membership consists of headquarters staff with interest in that particular program or functional area. The PEG chair was assigned from the staff agency that has the principal responsibility for either requirements determination or program development and performance within the established program or functional area. For example, in the case of the Modernization PEG, there were co-chairs, with the DCSOPS providing the manager for requirements and the ASA (RDA) providing the manager for program and performance. Staff representatives from offices of the DPA&E, the program sponsor, and the ASA (FM&C), usually the appropriation sponsor, serve as core members on each PEG. Other PEG members are from interested Army Headquarters staff elements. The PEG chairperson exercises ultimate decision authority for resource allocation but is charged with bringing unresolved issues to the PBC for review and guidance. PEG chairs are normally assigned to officers in the grade of colonel or their civilian equivalents from within their respective agencies.[5]

Council of Colonels

In the late 1980s, the DPA&E formalized the use of an ad hoc body called the COC to assist in execution and review of the programming function. The COC includes the PEG chairs or their representatives; the colonel-level representatives of the PBC members, including the colonels assigned to DPA&E and ASA (FM&C) as co-chairs; and for special subjects, colonels representing the interests of selected MACOMs or PEO/PMs. Since both PEGs and PBC memberships are represented on the COC, it provides a forum for discussing priorities, issues, resource allocation, program balance, and options for the complete program across all the PEGs. The COC conducts critical reviews of program presentations in preparation for reviews by the PBC and other PPBES review and guidance organs. The COC also serves an important role in disseminating program administrative guidance and information throughout the Army headquarters resource staff.

---

[5]AR 1-1, Sections 2-16 and 4-8, and Tables 1-4 and 1-5.

Major Army Commands and Program Executive Officers

The MACOMs are the principal field operating agencies, and the PEOs (and their subordinate materiel system Project Managers) are the principal acquisition agents of the Army. These two organizational groups provide inputs into the PPBES to establish requirements and obtain resources to conduct their separate activities. In the case of the MACOMs, they submit command budget estimates for resources; command plans for manpower and force structure; and more recently, command POMs to support programming. The PEOs oversee the research, development, and acquisition of major weapon systems and submit the program costings to support MDEPs for their respective systems. Throughout the programming phase, the MACOMs and PEO/PMs are informed of and respond to issues, resource allocation recommendations, and decisions at each level of the resource hierarchy. MACOM representatives are selectively invited to attend the PBC and COC as observers to assist in resolving issues.

Program and Budget Committee

The PBC is the Army's principal PPBES oversight and executive-advisory organization. It is composed of ARSTAF and Secretariat members, normally of general officer and SES rank. Its membership includes all program, resource, and requirements principals and selected functional areas with program, appropriation, or manpower oversight responsibility. It iteratively reviews the program, budget, and execution phases of PPBES; develops issues and options for Army leadership decisions; ensures consistency with policy and guidance; and recommends the draft program and budget estimate to more senior-level PPBES review and decisionmaking organizations.[6]

Prioritization Steering Group

The PSG is the next executive-level oversight and review organization senior to the PBC for the Army program process. The PSG is chaired

---

[6]AR 1-1, Section 2-14.

by the DCSOPS. It is composed primarily of ARSTAF member principals at the lieutenant general rank and selected invited participants from the Army Secretariat members at the assistant secretary rank with program or requirements management and oversight responsibilities. The DPA&E and the Director of the Army Budget participate in PSG deliberations and assure continuity of discussion. The PSG establishes priorities for major outstanding unfunded requirements and recommends funding sources to the ARB for a decision. It has specific responsibilities for developing options to solve critical unresourced requirements, ensuring consistency of priorities and guidance, and recommending issue decisions and an optimal integrated and balanced program for approval to the SELCOM (see AR 1-1, Section 2-14).

Select Committee

Until the changes made in 1995, the SELCOM was the senior executive review and integration organization at the Army Headquarters; it included both ARSTAF and Army Secretariat principals. The SELCOM was co-chaired by the USA and the VCSA. The principal purpose of the SELCOM was to provide oversight on all PPBES and major policy matters, review key issues, and recommend decisions to the Army senior leadership.[7]

Senior Army Decisionmakers

The senior Army leadership includes the Secretary of the Army, the CSA, the Under Secretary of the Army, and the VCSA. Key decisions are normally recommended to the CSA and Secretary by the VCSA and USA as the co-chairs of the SELCOM for joint consultation and decision. By law, the Secretary has the ultimate decision authority for Army functions. The Secretary of the Army, with the advice of the CSA, approves the Army POM.

---

[7]AR 1-1, Section 2-14.

THE ARMY PROGRAMMING PROCESS PRE-1995

Army programming is an ordered, event- and schedule-driven, hierarchical decision process. The process is centrally managed at the Army Headquarters with input from the MACOMs and PEOs that will ultimately execute the programs that Congress approves for funding in the budget. The formal programming process is normally initiated with senior Army leadership approval of TAP, which provides specific objectives, program priorities, and resource guidance for programming. TAP is developed within ODCSOPS through an iterative progressive process of coordinated staff inputs that develop the future strategic environment, implications for the Army, leadership guidance, and leadership decisions, including those from other major processes such as the Total Army Analysis (TAA), which results in decisions on the future force structure of the Army. The PEGs assist the development of TAP by providing their strategy supporting mid- and long-term objectives. These planning objectives are intended to guide the PEGs in their subsequent programming actions on resource allocation.

Subsequent to the publishing of TAP, the PEGs assigned MDEPs appropriate for their areas of responsibility. Generally, the assigned MDEPs in each PEG change little from one cycle to another and reflect changes in requirements and programs or shifts in staff interest or responsibility. The PEGs are provided data (in the form of PROBE Base File extracts) on the current resource positions and appropriate changes needed to prepare a baseline to begin the programming process. In addition to assignment of MDEPs, the PEGs receive guidance on their respective total allocations of resources (funding and manpower by fiscal years). Finally, DPA&E provides a schedule of events that requires the PEGs to reach decisions on resource allocation, provide input data reflection these actions to the PROBE database, and brief the PBC with an overview of their decisions, rationale, and remaining issues.

Each PEG resource allocation iteration is followed with a review by oversight organizations, such as the PBC, that give guidance to all the PEGs and adjust resource allocations among the PEGs to balance the broader Army program. After two or more iterations, the PBC review process identifies key resource issues (usually those requirements or programs that have not been allocated sufficient resources to achieve

their stated objectives), and potential sources for resource reallocation (lower priority programs that the PEGs have resourced), for discussion, guidance, and option development at a higher level.

Throughout the various iterations within the programming process,
the DPA&E is responsible for maintaining a current and timely
record of the resource allocation decisions (usually automated in the
PROBE database). The DPA&E is also empowered to analyze and
evaluate the activities of the PEGs and PBC, assist ODCSOPS in the
development of program options to respond to issues that are raised
to the PSG, SELCOM, and Army leadership, and oversee the balance
of resource decisions between competing requirements, programs,
and priorities.

The process progresses through the oversight hierarchy, with each
separate level attempting to winnow the issues until a small number
of remaining issues are presented to the Army leadership with recommendations for decision. It is normal practice within the Army to
reserve some unallocated resources for Army leadership use in their
final decisions to resolve outstanding issues. Options for addressing
the final few issues are provided, and decisions are normally made
that result in the resource allocation presented in the POM.[8]

The following sections discuss aspects of the Army programming
process in more detail.

MDEPs Record Program Requirements

Establishing the requirements to meet strategic military objectives
and departmental functions is fundamental to the programming
process. To enter the program process, requirements must have full
programmatic and fiscal descriptions, or MDEPs.

Any requirements sponsor in Army Headquarters may request
DPA&E to initiate MDEPs to support new requirements. In addition,
the DPA&E may assign requirements in MACOM POMs to separate
MDEPs to increase visibility. The DPA&E validates and approves the

---

[8]AR 1-1, Section 1-4.

assignment of MDEPs and provides oversight of all MDEPs through the PROBE database, which is used to manage all the MDEP records.

The collection of current MDEPs, representing programs in the current FYDP and as updated with congressional decisions on the current-year budget and OSD decisions on the next budget, is the initial resource baseline for initiating the programming process. Additional or new MDEPs representing emerging requirements are added to the existing MDEPs for resource consideration in the process. DPA&E assigns each MDEP and MDEP POC to one of the 14 PEGs, according to their appropriate functional or programmatic responsibilities, to validate requirements, interpret priorities, and allocate resources.

The MDEP is the Army's primary internal resource management tool. With final leadership decisions on resource allocation for the program, the collection of resourced MDEPs becomes the foundation of the Army's POM.

TAP Provides Initial Resource Guidance

The Army initiates the programming phase with Army leadership's approval of TAP. This document is normally issued in the fall of the year preceding the required delivery date of the POM to OSD. As the DPG does for the entire DoD, TAP gives the Army its resource priorities, major objectives, and program guidance. It also contains specific guidance sections for each of the PEGs (the Army Reserve and Army National Guard PEGs are excepted from this requirement in TAP but develop independently their objectives for programming). The PEG chairs normally write these respective guidance sections, which TAP proponents in DCSOPS integrate into a completed document. DPA&E works closely with DCSOPS to ensure that the resource guidance and priorities are sufficiently comprehensive and consistent with identified leadership positions and anticipated OSD guidance.

TAP has preceded the DPG by almost six months in recent years. This requires the DPA&E to issue periodic program guidance updates as draft iterations of the DPG arrive, concluding with the approved DPG and program Fiscal Guidance. In this regard, both the final DPG and OSD Fiscal Guidance generally are issued within six to eight weeks from the date the POM must be completed and delivered to OSD. Hence, while TAP provides an important benchmark to allow programming to proceed, there are important elements of subsequent guidance provided during the programming phase that may challenge aspects of TAP guidance.[9]

Program and Budget Links to Congress and the Warfighting CINCs

The Army also receives program input from other external sources. As mentioned earlier, the budget phase for the last submission to Congress is usually completed by December of the year prior to POM submission in May. Additionally, OMB and OSD provide all portions of DoD with the apportionment of the most recently approved congressional appropriation and authorization, usually between mid-November and late December, depending upon the timeliness of Congress. All these activities are of keen interest to those involved in programming. The actions taken on programs in the current and next budget years must be understood and feasibly continued during the program phase. DPA&E, in concert with the Director of the Army Budget, provides this information through the PROBE database to each MDEP POC. This ensures the connection from budget to program from the outset.

Each fall, the CINCs of the combatant commands submit their requirements in the form of IPLs through the CJCS to the Secretary of Defense. The IPLs are then distributed to the services for programmatic use. This becomes the link between requirements and resources for the operational commands. Normally, the Army receives IPLs after TAP is published, and the individual PEGs must consider them during their resource deliberations. TAP usually provides only general guidance on support for CINC requirements and does not establish separate priorities. DPA&E monitors those Army programs that relate to CINC IPLs throughout the programming process and assesses the corresponding program support provided to the CINCs by the Army POM.

---

[9]AR 1-1, Chapters 3 and 4.

Function of Programming Is to Allocate Resources to Requirements

The primary function of the programming process is to allocate resources to requirements that are represented programmatically by MDEPs. The ultimate goal of the programming process is to develop a feasible program, i.e., resources supporting a set of activities to accomplish a needed objective. In the aggregate, the total resources required to support all the Army's requirements generally exceed the expected fiscal allocation from OSD. Controls from other Army management processes, such as the Total Army Analysis process, constrain military force structure and selected other programs and often decide their respective resource allocation among the MDEPs. The DPA&E iteratively allocates fiscal guidance to the PEGs and requires them to further reallocate resources to their assigned MDEPs.[10] The PEGs program output is a listing of MDEPs in priority order for funding against their assigned fiscal guidance.

The PEGs have the basic responsibility to allocate resources to MDEPs. MDEPs can be resourced to meet their programmed requirements in full, in part, or not at all, depending on the decision of the PEGs as to the relative priority of the program(s) within an MDEP. MDEPs that are not resourced or only partially resourced by the PEGs are generally the basis for issues raised to the PBC. MDEPs that are given resources, in full or in part, and lack high priorities often become the sources of funding for remaining resource issues. In the iterative cycles that this draft programming follows, many of the MDEPs that deal with funds will be selectively reduced below total program requirements. For example, for modernization MDEPs, the system quantities to be procured within one or more of the FYDP years may be reduced, along with a commensurate reduction in funds. Conversely, the MDEPs recording the military force structure for organizations seldom change during programming as they were decided in advance by the Army leadership within the TAA process.

---

[10]DPA&E apportions the expected fiscal guidance between the 14 PEGs based upon an estimate of the value of the highest-priority MDEPs assigned. This is an iterative process that is not finalized until the receipt of OSD Fiscal Guidance. Normally, the DPA&E withholds a small bank of resources to support Army leadership decisions, often amounting to between $0.5 and $1.0 billion per year over the FYDP. This bank is normally used to broker the final POM issue decisions.

The Program and Budget Committee Reviews the Output of the PEGs

The programming efforts of the PEGs are generally driven by schedule. The PEGs are required to input data to PROBE to record their initial and subsequent resource allocations, which are followed by briefings of program status and issues to the PBC. The DPA&E reviews the total program for balance, meeting TAP guidance, and issue identification. In conjunction with the PEG briefings, the DPA&E reviews the overall program with the PBC. The PBC provides supplementary guidance to each PEG on specific issues, and the DPA&E may reassign MDEPs and reallocate resources to the PEGs for the next iteration. This process of resource allocation, issue identification, review, and adjustment of guidance usually proceeds for three or more cycles of PBC involvement.

The principal function of the PBC is to reduce the number of issues through a process of tradeoffs among MDEPs, both within and between PEGs, that provide a rough balance of resources to priority requirements. This portion of the programming process concludes with the PBC endorsing a select set of major program issues and recommending the resulting allocation of resources to the next-higher review organ, the PSG, for its consideration and guidance. Thereafter, the PBC continues to be informed of the actions of higher review organizations and occasionally is tasked to consider a specific issue and provide options and recommendations to higher bodies, such as the PSG and SELCOM. Additionally, the PBC continues to function throughout the program phase as a discussion forum and source of information for the headquarters staff and selected invited MACOMs.

Draft Programs for Review and Option Development

The PSG and SELCOM review the programming results of the PEGs and PBC. However, the PSG is normally the most senior organ to resolve issues and adjust resources in the program on the basis of priorities. The PSG primarily involves the application of senior military judgment to develop options for solving the remaining issues. The PSG usually reduces the number of issues by making fiscal adjustments that the DCSOPS determines based upon the priorities of competing requirements. The appropriate PEGs implement guidance received from the PSG and record it in PROBE; the resulting draft program is presented to the SELCOM with any remaining issues intended for resolution by the Army leadership.

Normally, the PBC reviews the output of the PSG to ensure a full understanding of how priorities affect resource allocation in the program. Issues not raised at the PSG may be developed in the SELCOM based upon the expanded perspectives of the Army Secretariat membership. This final SELCOM review allows an opportunity any final issues to be explored prior to the program briefing to the senior Army leadership.

The SELCOM (and beginning in 1995, the ARB) provides a senior-level forum of both military and civilian staff leaders for final discussion of the draft program and issues in the presence of the CSA and the Secretary of the Army. In rare cases, issues briefed to the SELCOM are solved through the mediation and eventual unanimity of the members. Since the SELCOM has no decision authority over the program resources withheld for the senior Army leadership, it normally endorses the draft program and remaining issues as received from the PSG and recommends an allocation of funding from the Army leadership's resource bank. The SELCOM is the last and most senior formal organ to review the draft POM prior to the final decisions of the Army leadership.

Final Program Decisions

Subsequent to the SELCOM review and recommendations, the CSA and Secretary of the Army are briefed on the draft POM. There are usually a number of separate informal interim reviews for the CSA and the Secretary during the programming phase. Each discusses the outstanding issues and options for solution with their principal advisers and, where applicable, MACOM commanders. The CSA and Secretary often conduct private discussions to exchange views and information prior to a final decision. In addition to solving outstanding issues, the Army leadership is also concerned with the balance of the entire program, issues that will be raised to OSD, and strategies to improve their program and fiscal posture. These items give focus to final decisions on resource allocation that yields the basis for the Army POM.

Completion of the POM

The POM is a comprehensive document with voluminous data and narrative that responds to requirements stated in the DoD Program Preparation Instructions (PPI). There are two major portions to the POM. The first is the narrative that provides a strategic justification for how resources were allocated and usually highlights major program achievements and unresolved issues. The narrative addresses the Army's objectives on a functional and detailed basis articulating the Army's program responses to OSD guidance. The second major portion of the POM consists of the tabular data displayed quantitatively, that relate the detailed resource allocations among programs in format prescribed by OSD in the PPI.

In the final analysis, the POM consists of a collection of MDEPs that are synthesized among Army themes.[11] In general, the Army POM did not attempt to link to the joint operational requirements; rather, it noted the resource applied to joint requirements after the resourcing decisions had been made. Thus, the joint requirements served as a scorecard type of assessment against which the Army could measure the amount of joint requirements that it had met in its POM.

Decisions on resource allocation are coupled with their corresponding rationales and linked to the strategy, objectives, and priorities from TAP and DPG with an assessment of their expected outputs. Sections focus on the major Defense Program categories and highlight resource support for selected programs, such as the CINC IPLs. The Army often provides an appendix identifying critical shortfalls and program issues to justify the allocation of additional resources by OSD. The DPA&E oversees, compiles, and edits the inputs from staff elements and PEGs and writes the executive summary of the POM. Subsequently, the DPA&E develops the POM briefing, an overview of resource allocation and key issues, which is then presented to the Defense Resources Board (DRB), the JS, and the CINCs. Receipt of the POMs, usually in May, signals the beginning of the DoD program review and issue cycle, which is conducted throughout most of the summer.

---

[11]Following the implementation of the modified framework, the Army found it easier to satisfy itself that the POM reflected resource objectives that were based upon joint requirements, not merely a reflection of internal Army requirements.

STRATEGY-TO-TASKS RESOURCE MANAGEMENT FRAMEWORK

DEVELOPING A STRATEGY-TO-TASKS RESOURCE MANAGEMENT FRAMEWORK

The STRM framework,[1] developed at RAND during the late 1980s, is a decision-support process for linking resources to the National Security Strategy. It is included in this analysis because it forms a backdrop for the assessment of functions and tasks. If used correctly, the framework links resource decisions to specific military tasks that require resources, which in turn are linked hierarchically to higher-level operational and national security objectives. The framework establishes the downward connection from strategies to programs and tasks, as well as the upward connection from tasks up through strategies. As defined by Goldwater-Nichols, the CINCs are the demanders of resources because they perform the operational missions and tasks. The services and defense agencies are the suppliers, providing resources or functional capabilities to the demanders. The adjudicators (integrators) are the OSD and Chairman, as assigned by the legislation.

Figure B.1 illustrates the STRM operational framework. At the highest levels of the hierarchy, we consider **national goals**. The national goals form the basis for all U.S. statements on national security.

---

[1]The framework used in this analysis is essentially the same as that being used by the Joint Staff for JWCA analysis and by a number of DoD organizations. The objectives, strategies, and tasks identified here are based on discussions with the Joint Staff, the services, and the CINCs on the current articulation of the national security and national military strategies. The specifics of the structure continue to evolve. This appendix describes the framework as it was configured in 1995.

National security objectives include political, economic, military, and diplomatic objectives necessary to protect and defend the United States and its interests around the world. In contrast to national goals, national security objectives change in accordance with changes in the geopolitical environment. **National military objectives** define what must be done to preserve and protect our fundamental principles, goals, and interests with respect to threats and challenges.

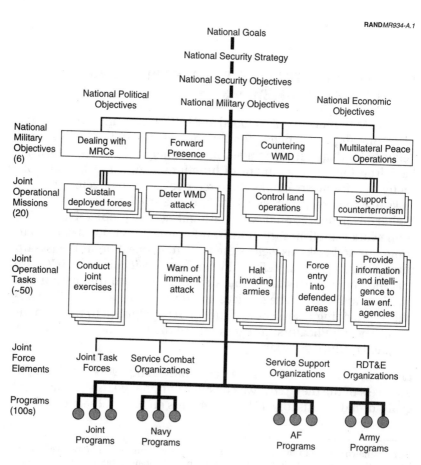

Figure B.1—STRM Operational Framework

Joint operational missions are attained by a combatant commander within a concept of operations or a campaign plan to accomplish his mission.[2]

Joint operational tasks define various military strategies. They describe how forces will be used to support the national military objectives and define the military strategy for a particular region. A particular regional military strategy is defined within the framework of the national military strategy and from the Secretary's and Chairman's guidance. Functional objectives indicate the support activities that must be present to sustain any military operation.

Military support functions are the activities on the supply side of the defense resources equation that underpin all operational missions. These functions are derived from law but are specified most clearly in DoD Directive 5100.1, "Functions of the Department of Defense and Its Major Components."

Military support tasks are the supply-side activities performed to accomplish military support functions. They decompose the broader functional assignments of DoD Directive 5100.1 into more manageable pieces for assessment. Like joint operational tasks, they may be linked to more than one higher-level objective.

Force elements are the sets of resources that are used to accomplish tasks. These can be standing Joint Task Forces with members from more than one service or more traditional units, such as Army or Marine battalions, Air Force squadrons, or Navy ships. The appropriate force elements to consider in assessing the capability of forces are determined by consideration of a concept of operations for accomplishing an operational mission.

Programs are the ultimate focus of resource decisions. The adequacy of funding and the timing of new force elements or systems entering the inventory can only be assessed by considering the missions that they support and the alternative programs that can provide capabilities that meet the same objectives. Programs are linked, through force elements, to both the supply side and the demand side of our framework. For example, budgets are prepared by the services

---

[2]See Pirnie (1996) for the most recent formulations and detailed definitions.

as a "supply-side" support function and include funding to support a specific number of units with a standard set of equipment. How the number of units meets national requirements requires linkage of programs up through the "demand-side" joint operational missions that those programs and units support. Consideration of both sides is necessary for program integration.

BUILDING THE CURRENT STRM FRAMEWORK

The change of administrations in 1993 required reviewing the elements of the STRM framework for consistency with the emerging policies and priorities of President Clinton. Official public statements and published materials[3] were used to evaluate what changes, if any, occurred in our national security policies. As expected, there were no changes in the national goals. Despite a change in terminology for the National Security Strategy—*A National Security Strategy of Engagement and Enlargement* (Clinton, 1995)—the political, economic, military, and diplomatic activities deemed necessary to achieve U.S. wartime and peacetime national security objectives remained the same. However, there were shifts in emphasis from the use of military force to increased utilization of diplomatic, interagency, and cooperative efforts to thwart threats to our national security. The basic operational framework is shown in Figure B.1.[4] The national security objectives also did not change significantly, but again there is increased emphasis on cooperative defense initiatives, particularly in the Third World (The White House, 1994). From the Clinton administration's documents, we discern the following national security objectives and associated tasks or regions of interest:

- Enhancing Our Security

    — Maintain a strong defense capability

    — Decide when and how to employ U.S. forces

    — Combat the spread and use of weapons of mass destruction and missiles

---

[3]The public statements of the President, SECDEF, and the CJCS.

[4]These are the demands placed on military forces.

- — Support arms control
- — Participate in peace operations
- — Maintain strong intelligence capabilities
- — Protect and improve the environment

- Promoting Prosperity at Home
  - — Enhance American competitiveness
  - — Create partnerships with business and labor
  - — Enhance access to foreign markets
  - — Strengthen macroeconomic conditions
  - — Provide for energy security
  - — Promote sustainable development abroad

- Promoting Democracy
  - — Cooperate with other democracies
  - — Enlarge community of democratic and free-market nations

- Regional Security Objectives
  - — Attain economic cooperation and democratization in

- Europe and Eurasia
- East Asia and the Pacific
- The Western Hemisphere
- Africa
- The Middle East, Southwest and South Asia.

National Military Objectives

Typically, national military objectives are drawn directly from the national military strategy.[5] The six military objectives we discern are

- Deal with major regional conflicts
- Provide a credible overseas presence
- Counter weapons of mass destruction
- Contribute to multilateral peace operations
- Support counterterrorism efforts and other national security objectives
- Maintain joint readiness.

Joint Operational Missions

The national military objectives must rationally link up to the national security objectives and down to the more operationally focused military missions. Operational missions differ from military objectives in that they are the "how to do" or description of the various elements of a military objective. Joint operational missions provide the crosswalk from the policy objectives contained in the upper tiers of the hierarchy (see Figure B.1) to the operational and resource elements, or the lower tiers. The joint operational missions are what we call the "spine" or backbone of the framework. The list of joint operational missions below has evolved from examination of operational plans and military science by RAND analysts and military professionals. Alternative formulations are possible, but the current list of 20 operational missions captures all of the operations envisioned in the National Security Strategy (and the national military strategy document). They were fleshed out according to each national military objective. Although operational missions could cross military objectives, we initially identified a supporting list of opera-

---

[5]We drew from *A National Security Strategy of Engagement and Enlargement,* July 1994, because the new national military strategy document had not been released at the time of the analysis. The national military strategy released in February 1995 reflects the same objectives.

tional missions for each military objective. The joint operational missions we identified are

- Control weapons of mass destruction
- Rapidly transport and sustain an overwhelming force
- Control enemy ability to initiate and sustain combat operations
- Control land operations
- Control maritime operations
- Control air operations
- Control space operations
- Control information/intelligence operations
- Conduct routine training operations in forward areas
- Sustain forward deployed forces
- Maintain prepositioned equipment and stocks
- Deter hostile major powers from attacking with weapons of mass destruction
- Prevent/deter/defeat attacks from other hostile nations with weapons of mass destruction
- Control ability to acquire, produce, or employ weapons of mass destruction
- Participate in traditional peace operations
- Participate in multinational peacekeeping operations
- Support humanitarian activities
- Support counterterrorism efforts
- Provide domestic military support
- Support other national missions.

Joint Operational Tasks

With the identification and agreement on the first five tiers of the hierarchy—national goals, National Security Strategy, national security goals, national military objectives, and joint operational missions—we turned to the operational tasks. For example, in the U.S. Southern Command and U.S. Forces Korea (USFK) applications of the STRM, we identified tasks that were unique to those commands. The post–Desert Shield/Desert Storm environment stresses joint operations and the need for the services to compete for key roles in joint operational missions and for associated resources.[6] Thus, all tasks were defined within the context of joint operational tasks. The tasks are not service specific. Tasks were iteratively identified by consulting published literature on the various military roles and missions, consulting with experts in the area of joint operations, and debate among the project team, which contained members with service and joint staff experience.[7] Forty-eight joint operational tasks were identified, along with many subtasks; they range from concept and doctrine formulation to the provision of disaster relief. Examples of the joint operational tasks are listed below:

- Formulate concepts, doctrine, and requirements

- Conduct joint exercises

- Maintain stationed forces

- Rapidly transport military forces and material into and within theater

- Evict enemy force from critical areas

- Destroy/disrupt enemy information and intelligence operations.

---

[6]The concept of competition among the military departments for missions and roles has been further substantiated in Congress' formation of the Commission on Roles and Missions.

[7]The manuals consulted were FM 100-5, *Operations*, June 14, 1993; FM 100-1, *The Army*, December 1991; and the *Universal Joint Task List*, CJCSM 3500.04, May 1995.

REPORTING RESOURCE ALLOCATIONS

The functional PEGs were required to report their resource allocations to the PBC during the POM build using the following briefing formats. These formats focused on assessments of resourcing at the objective levels (See A, P, and U below), summarized assessments of resource tasks within priority groupings (I, II, and III), any identified resource issues, and an overall assessment of the capability to accomplish the function in both the near- and mid-terms (budget years and program years, respectively). Use of common presentations allowed the PBC to identify cross-cutting issues, to determine potential sources for issue resolution, and to develop a sense of the program balance across the six functions. Subsequently, the PBC issued guidance to the PEGs to make resource allocation adjustments that will address many of the identified but unresolved resource issues.

The PEGs were asked to assess their allocation of the resources assigned to them. An assessment scale was devised to score each resource task. The assessments were included with other information entered in the spreadsheets corresponding to the decisions supporting PROBE data inputs for POM File 1.0. In addition to the assessments, those resource tasks that were not changed from the original resource baseline (in 1996, this was PROBE Base File 3.0) were listed as *No Change.* The three possible assessments are as follows:

- **A:** *Adequately* resourced to ensure all validated requirements of this task can be accomplished.

- **P:** *Partially* resourced but will not accomplish all validated requirements of this task.

- **U:** *Unfunded* and validated requirements of this task will not be accomplished.

Resource task priorities consider, at the highest level, the *relative* importance across all functions of the Army, and at other levels, the *relative* importance within a specific functional area or PEG. The priorities are in four hierarchical groupings but are not directly related to specific resourcing levels (i.e., there are no established minimum amounts or percentages of funding required by a priority, and priorities do not direct a specific hierarchy of resources). These priorities also address the criticality and associated risk of an activity *relative* to other activities. The risk to the achievement of Army goals and resource objectives is also a direct consideration within these priorities, with higher priorities having little margin for risk and lower priorities having increased risk. For instance, a Priority III task could be resourced fully, since partial resourcing might produce excessive risk (e.g., breach a contract threshold). The priorities are shown below:

- **Priority I:** These tasks are of fundamental importance to the overall achievement of the specified goals of the Army as an institution (*not* the individual components or commands within the Army, such as the Training and Doctrine Command [TRADOC]). These tasks have a major effect on the Army's role of providing for the operational needs of the CINCs. The tasks are generally enduring, and their achievement is directly related to the objectives of the NMS. Tasks assigned this priority are the most important to the Army leadership, and very little risk to their achievement should be accepted.

- **Priority II:** These tasks are important to the achievement of the key resource objectives within a primary function of the Army (Man, Equip, Train, etc.). These tasks either broadly or directly support the principal elements of their related function and are considered critical to its achievement over the long term. There should be low risk associated with the achievement of these tasks.

- **Priority III:** These tasks are important to enabling some portion or subsystem of a primary function of the Army. These tasks are supportive of narrow aspects of resource objectives. Their achievement usually supports or enables a key resource subobjective of that function. There should be no more than moderate risk associated with the achievement of these tasks.

- **Priority IV:** These tasks are of lesser importance (i.e., not Priorities I–III) and require either program visibility (i.e., in response to Army, OSD, CINC, or congressional special interest or directed guidance), close coordination among more than one PEG, or exchange of resource information among one or more staff agencies and MACOMs.[1] They can be related to one or more primary functions of the Army or a number of key resource objectives. Generally, these tasks do not pose any significant risk to the achievement of the overall Army goals or key resource objectives.

---

[1]It should be noted that the Priority IV tasks have subsequently been replaced by Priority 0 tasks that require multiple PEG coordination or special visibility and are not ranked according to their strict resource priority (i.e., Priority I–III).

Figure C.1—Overview of Resource Objectives

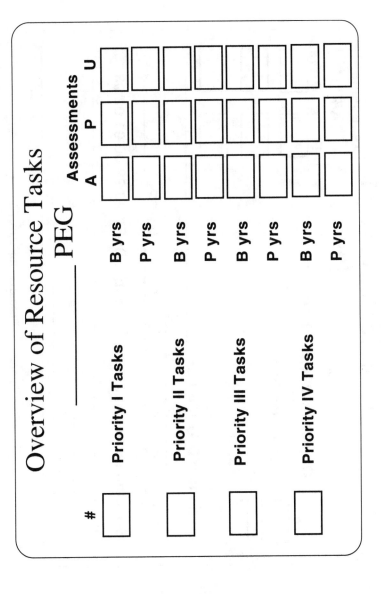

Figure C.2—Overview of Resource Tasks

RAND*MR934-C.3*

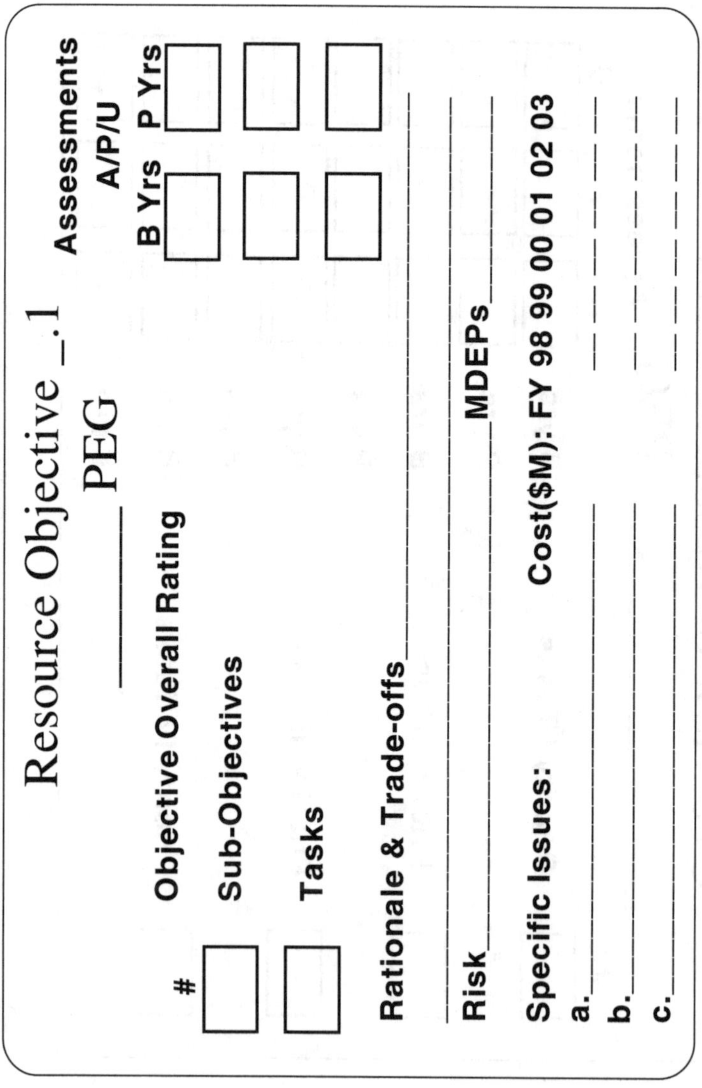

Resource Objective _.1

PEG ____

Assessments

A/P/U

B Yrs P Yrs

Objective Overall Rating

\#

Sub-Objectives

Tasks

Rationale & Trade-offs ____

Risk ____

MDEPs ____

Specific Issues: **Cost($M): FY 98 99 00 01 02 03**

a. ____

b. ____

c. ____

Figure C.3—Resource Objective_.1

RANDMR934-C.1

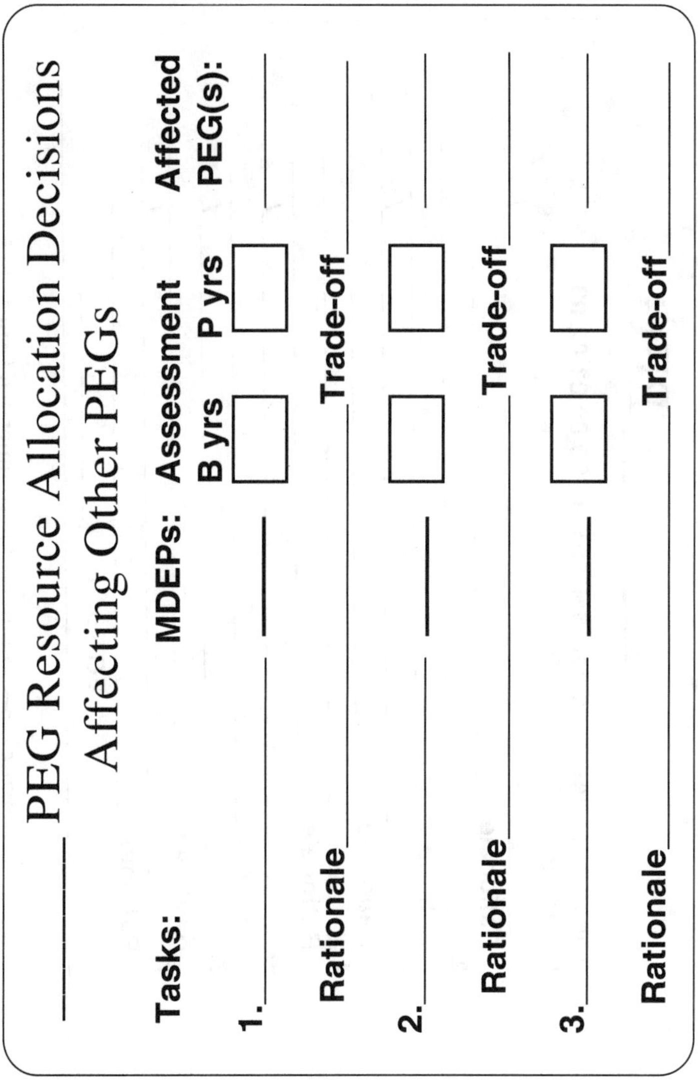

PEG Resource Allocation Decisions
Affecting Other PEGs

Tasks: MDEPs: Assessment   Affected
                                                    PEG(s):

                           B yrs   P yrs

1. _____   _____   [ ]   [ ]   _____

Rationale _____ Trade-off _____

2. _____   _____   [ ]   [ ]   _____

Rationale _____ Trade-off _____

3. _____   _____   [ ]   [ ]   _____

Rationale _____ Trade-off _____

Figure C.4—PEG Resource Allocation Decisions Affecting Other PEGs

RANDMR934-C.5

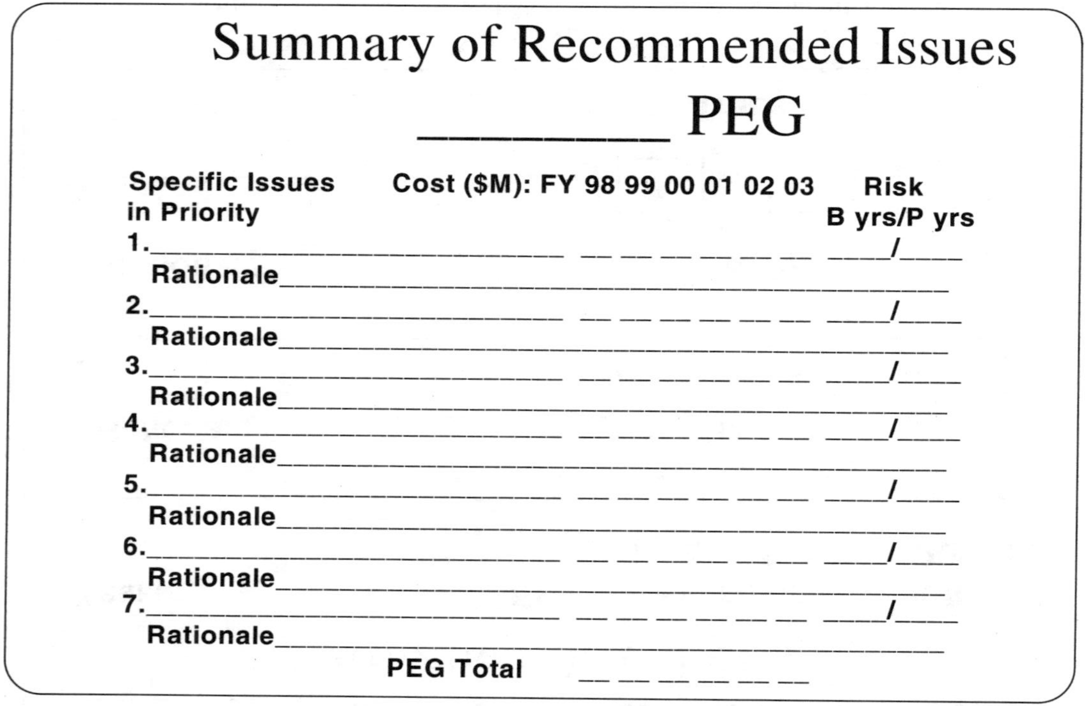

Figure C.5—Summary of Recommended Issues

BIBLIOGRAPHY

Chairman of the Joint Chiefs of Staff, *Universal Joint Task List,* CJCSM 3500.04, May 1995.

Clinton, William, *A National Security Strategy of Engagement and Enlargement,* Washington, D.C.: The White House, February 1995.

The Commission on the Roles and Missions of the Armed Forces of the United States, *Directions for Defense,* Washington, D.C.: U.S. Government Printing Office, May 1995.

Lewis, Leslie, and C. Robert Roll, *Strategy-to-Tasks: A Methodology for Resource Allocation and Management,* Santa Monica, CA: RAND, P-7839, 1993.

Lewis, Leslie, James A. Coggin, and C. Robert Roll, *The United States Special Operations Command Resource Management Process: An Application of the Strategy-to-Tasks Framework,* Santa Monica, CA: RAND, MR-445-A/SOCOM, 1994.

Lewis, Leslie, Preston Niblack, William Schwabe, and John Schrader, *Overseas Presence: Joint Warfighting Capabilities Assessment Conference,* Santa Monica, CA: RAND, PM-359-JS, 1995.

Lewis, Leslie, C. Robert Roll, and Ronald E. Sortor, Bernard Rostker, *Organizational Analysis and Resource Management Planning: An-notated Briefing,* Santa Monica, CA: RAND, N-3313-A, 1993.

Lewis, Leslie, John Schrader, William Schwabe, C. Robert Roll, and Ralph Suarez, *USFK Strategy-to-Task Resource Management: A*

Framework for Resource Decisionmaking, Santa Monica, CA: RAND, MR-654-USFK, 1996.

Lewis, Leslie, John Schrader, William A. Schwabe, Roger A. Brown, *Joint Warfighting Capabilities (JWCA) Integration, Report on Phase 1 Research*, Santa Monica, CA: RAND, MR-872-JS, 1998.

Pirnie, Bruce, *An Objectives-Based Approach to Military Campaign Analysis*, Santa Monica, CA: RAND, MR-656-JS, 1996.

Public Law 99-433 October 1, 1986.

U.S. Army, After-Action Report, July 8, 1996.

U.S. Army, *Operations*, FM 100-5, June 14, 1993.

U.S. Army, *The Army*, FM 100-1, December 1991.

U.S. Army War College, *Army Command, Leadership, and Management: Theory and Practice, 1995–1996*, Carlisle Barracks, PA, June 1995.

U.S. Department of the Army, *Army Regulation 1-1: Planning, Programming, Budgeting, and Execution System*, January 30, 1994.

The White House, *A National Security Strategy of Engagement and Enlargement*, July 1994.